The uncertain power

The uncertain power

A political history of the United States since 1929

Robert Garson and Christopher J. Bailey

Manchester University Press

Manchester and New York

distributed exclusively in the USA and Canada by St. Martin's Press

Published by Manchester University Press
Oxford Road, Manchester M13 9PL, UK
and Room 400, 175 Fifth Avenue,
New York, NY 10010, USA

Distributed exclusively in the USA and Canada
by St. Martin's Press, Inc.,
175 Fifth Avenue, New York, NY 10010, USA

British Library cataloguing in publication data
Garson, Robert
  The uncertain power: a political history of the United States since 1929.
  1. United States, 1901–
  I. Title II. Bailey, Christopher J.
  973.9

Library of Congress cataloging in publication data
Garson, Robert A.
      The uncertain power: a political history of the United States
    since 1929 / Robert Garson and Christopher J. Bailey.
        p.   cm.
    Includes index.
    ISBN 0-7190-2686-5
    1. United States – Politics and government – 20th century.
  2. United States – Foreign relations – 20th century.
  I. Bailey, Christopher J. II. Title
  E743.G34 1990
  973.9—dc20   90-39740

ISBN 0 7190 2686 5 *hardback*
     0 7190 2687 3 *paperback*

Typeset in Galliard by
Koinonia Ltd, Manchester
Printed in Great Britain by
Biddles Ltd, King's Lynn and Guildford

Contents

Preface and acknowledgements *page* vii

1 The Great Crash as prologue, 1929-1932   1
2 The New Deal, 1933-1940   8
3 The US and the Second World War, 1939-1945   20
4 The politics of reconversion, 1945-1952   37
5 The origins of the Cold War, 1945-1952   52
6 Years of affluence, 1952-1960   67
7 Foreign policy in the Eisenhower era, 1953-1960   79
8 Towards a Great Society, 1961-1968   93
9 Foreign policy in the Democratic years, 1961-1968   104
10 Years of stagflation, 1968-1980   119
11 From detente to national malaise, 1969-1980   131
12 The new Republican era, 1981-1990   143

Index   157

Preface and acknowledgements

This book has, we think, a modest goal. There are dozens of textbooks on American history and new additions can often just add to the clutter. We are aware, however, that British students of recent America or of America's role in international affairs do not have ready access to short histories of the United States since the Great Depression. The last ten years or so have seen some dramatic shifts in world politics and in the distribution of the world's wealth. The Cold War seems no longer a fixture of international life and the emerging nations in the Asian Pacific are serious contenders in world trade.

This has inevitably led historians to reassess the recent past. This is a modest contribution to that reassessment. We do not pretend to have written a comprehensive history. There is little in this book on demographic change, popular culture, feminism and many ethnic minorities. We do not under-estimate their significance. We have simply sought to provide a short political history of the United States since 1929 and for that reason our attention is focused on the national political agenda. Thus the concentration on such matters as civil rights, the anticommunist crusade, social reform and foreign policy is dictated by the fact that so much energy was consumed by the White House and Congress on these matters.

Even within these confines we have restricted our discussions. Brevity has its price, but it concentrates the mind. We have attempted to provide a reasonably comprehensive overview but have reserved more detailed discussion for those issues that lingered and moulded public policy in future years. Thus, for example, our discussion of military strategy in the Second World War concentrates on those arenas that were to affect the development of the Cold War. We hope that this volume will be read as a series of essays on recent America and not just as a broad survey. If students read this book, decide that there is more to the story, and then scour libraries for more detail, we will be more than content.

We owe thanks to a number of people. Karen Harrison did not just help with the typing, but was both a critic and choreographer of a *pas de deux* that spanned the Atlantic Ocean. Richard Purslow of Manchester University Press waited patiently while we hiccupped. Our colleagues in the David Bruce Centre for American Studies at the University of Keele provided the convivial environment that is so essential to all scholarship. Finally we would like to extend some personal thanks. Robert Garson has been cheered throughout his parenthood by Sonia and Adrian. They are not just loving children; as they approach adulthood, they have become great friends. Vicki, his wife, provided all the encouragement he could have dreamt of and more. She supported this effort when it was needed; and distracted him superbly when the need for that distraction became overwhelming. If it were possible to dedicate a book that is jointly authored, it would be dedicated to her. Chris Bailey has been supported throughout the writing of this book by his wife Mandy. Not only has her encouragement helped to overcome some early obstacles and frustrations, but her love has helped to sustain him during a period of much change.

The Great Crash as prologue, 1929-1932

As the decade of the 1920s was drawing to an end Americans had good reason to bask in self-congratulation. They had emerged from the First World War as the world's greatest financial and creditor nation. Their manufacturing output, production of food, extent of technological innovation and stock of gold surpassed all their competitors. There was, as the historian William Leuchtenburg has commented, 'the contagious feeling that everyone was meant to get rich'. President Calvin Coolidge, in his last message to Congress in December 1928, stated that there had never been a 'more pleasing prospect than that which appears at the present time. In the domestic field there is tranquility and contentment ... and the highest record of years of prosperity.' Americans felt good about themselves. Real per capita income had risen by almost one-third in a decade. Businessmen were satisfied with their profit margins, workers were broadly content with their moderate gains in earnings. Easy credit, a drop in the real cost of consumer durables, tax reductions and the odd windfall profit from dealing in stocks meant that automobiles, household appliances, and leisure pursuits were within the reach of the vast majority of gainfully employed people. There were problems, but then there always are. There has never been a time, in any nation's history, when everybody has enjoyed the fruits of life equally. Someone always misses out. Blacks suffered discrimination, farmers could not keep up with urban prosperity because of low farm prices and wage levels in older industries lagged behind. But broad judgements have to be made about the total picture, and on balance times were good. Between 1921 and 1929 industrial production had almost doubled. In 1929 the United States produced about five million motor vehicles, about ten times the total equivalent production of Britain, France and Germany combined. Its total output exceeded that of the other six great powers taken together. The newer industries produced for the home. Radios, refrigerators, wristwatches,

Pyrex glass, canned foods and, of course, motor cars were easily and cheaply available. The fruits of prosperity surrounded everybody, and were not just a series of statistics.

A further reason for smugness lay in the United States' role in the wider world. Despite large increases in imports and exports, the United States was relatively self-sufficient. Only 8 per cent of its manufactured goods were exported abroad. The rest of the world did not hold the key to American prosperity. American factories produced for American demand. If things could stay that way, it was reasoned, the United States would be largely immune to economic upheaval abroad. The high tariffs adopted by the United States in the 1920s were partly motivated by the belief that international trade in goods was relatively unimportant. Even though it was a creditor nation and needed imports, it was happy to choke off trade. The United States maintained its economic position by private investment of American dollars abroad. American capital built factories in Europe, drilled oil wells in the Middle East and developed plantations in the Far East. Americans believed that their prosperity and their investments could be best defended by taking a guarded and cautious role in world affairs. The United States needed raw materials and a political climate that was hospitable to investment. It insisted on stability among its Latin American neighbours. It believed that it could best further its interests by promoting business, by ensuring that international debt payments were scheduled in an orderly fashion, and that naval rivalry was brought under control through the treaty-making process.

There seemed to be no major threat to American interests in the 1920s: while old European rivalries died hard, they did little to challenge American supremacy. The United States was happy with the status quo. Its dedication to fashionable schemes to freeze naval armaments and to pledges of non-aggression was based on the optimistic belief that other nations were happy as things were, too. Power had shifted to the United States almost too quickly. There was little inclination for bold strokes. Attitudes do not change overnight. The pursuit of short-term economic advantage seemed to make sense. Few Americans were prepared to risk the use of military power for maintaining the world order or deterring other nations from upsetting the status quo.

The era of self-congratulation came to an unpleasant end in the great stock market crash of October 1929 and the general financial collapse that followed in its wake. Soaring share prices, the bull market, had caught a grip on life in the late 1920s. It took little skill to make money on the stock market. Share prices rose spectacularly and seldom reflected the individual performance of the company concerned. Share prices had been rising almost without a blip since early 1927. In that year the *New York Times* average index of industrial stocks had risen 69 points, nearly 40 per cent. Anyone with money believed they could not afford to stay on the sidelines. Why wait a week, when stock prices would only be higher? If a man was a little short of spare cash, he could borrow, buy more stock, and then use that stock as collateral to buy still more stock. America was in the grip of a spiralling speculative frenzy. During 1928 shares in Radio went up from 85 points to 420; Montgomery Ward went up from 117 to 440. The *New York Times* industrial average gained 86 points, a further 35 per cent. Getting rich never seemed easier. The bubble was destined to burst. Stock prices must either reflect company performance or they should be a measure of anticipated future growth. Company profits had not grown at the same spectacular rate and all the indicators pointed to a decrease in demand, if only because many industrial companies had overproduced and had created stockpiles of unwanted goods. The realization dawned in the late summer of 1929. In early September the bull market broke. In October matters got worse. Panic struck and the scramble to sell began in earnest. Then on Tuesday, 29 October 1929, a date that J. K.Galbraith has called 'the most devastating day in the history of markets', the great plunge began. Large blocks of stocks were sold for whatever price somebody cared to pay. By the end of the day all the gains of the preceding year had been wiped out. Individual investors had lost fortunes. Banks and corporations recalled their money. Those who had borrowed to buy stock now had to pay for paper that had plummeted in value.

The shock of the stock market crash to the economy was indescribable. Normally, stock market fluctuations do not cause business fluctuations, but the Great Crash was an exception. People were required to reimburse the money borrowed for their speculations. The supply of investment funds was reduced and money for domestic consumption just evaporated. Worse still was the structural weakness of the banking system. There were waves of bank failures as depositors withdrew funds. Many of the banks were too small. They had been required to provide their own liquidity and they simply could not. Often tied to one small community, they lacked staying power and folded. Individual Federal reserve banks had allowed member-bank reserves to fall drastically and the money supply began to contract at an accelerated rate. Currency was being withdrawn internally by depositors and gold was being withdrawn externally by foreigners. Interest rates were raised sharply, but these exacerbated the banks' difficulties, and further runs occurred.

The economy started to go to pot. The gross national product, the total of goods and services produced, declined from $104.4 billion in 1929 to $74.2 billion in 1933. Wholesale prices declined by one-third. In the same period civilian employment dropped by nearly 20 per cent. Unemployment rose from 3.1 per cent of the labour force in 1929 to about one quarter in 1933. The figures do not convey the despair. Depressions had happened before, and to begin with Americans hoped they could sit it out and that it would go away. But the depression of the 1930s did not behave as Americans believed depressions should behave. Each year the situation got worse. Manufacturing output did not reach its 1929 level until late 1936, and even then that was not accompanied by a comparable improvement in employment. The figures do not tell us how long people were unemployed. They do not tell us how many workers took jobs that were below their demonstrated capacity. They do not tell us whether earnings were sufficient to provide decent diet and shelter. Bank failures devastated those who had entrusted their savings to the banks. Some people even found that although they had lost all their savings, they still had to continue to repay loans from the same bank. Farmers fared no better. Farm prices fell 61 per cent between 1929 and 1933. Farmers found that it was sometimes cheaper to destroy their crops than to pay the transportation fees to get those crops to market. Housing standards declined. People could not afford repairs. Rented accommodation was too expensive, and the only solution was sometimes to double up with another family. There was the cruel paradox of a good housing stock, with many houses and apartments lying empty, while others were overcrowded. Family ties were fragile. Stress increased family conflict. Others just took to the roads, using either their old cars or jumping trains. Of course, people survived. They were hungry, but few died directly of hunger. Common hardship creates its own bonds. Individuals were determined to weather the storm, and even those on the margins of society, such as the nomadic sharecroppers and the 'Okies', refugees of the dustbowl, reportedly found a sense of cameraderie. It was such bonds that Franklin Roosevelt, elected President in 1932, would so skilfully nurture.

As the depression deepened in the early 1930s Americans began to question whether capitalism and the American system of government would cope with the crisis in faith as well as the more practical matter of stopping the downward slide. The Republican President, Herbert Hoover, was convinced that the United States was facing one of those periodic downward business cycles that rear their head from time to time. He did not fiddle while the United States burned, but he did believe that the crisis would eventually resolve itself. Until such a resolution occurred, he hoped to use government power and suasion to prop up the economy. He used that power hesitantly and reluctantly. His misgivings were partly ideological and partly the result of his inexperience as a politician. He genuinely believed that the prosperity of the 1920s had been due to the special economic climate of the United States, and that government involvement could become inextricable and would prevent the eventual restoration of a sound economy. He began by trying to persuade business leaders to maintain wage rates in order to prevent a further shrinkage of purchasing power. When that failed – business simply could not afford to maintain wage and employment levels in a shrinking market – he urged state and local governments to increase spending and created national committees to solicit private funds for unemployment relief. Private charity was almost useless; it did not have national networks of distribution and anyway it could not raise the money. Hoover almost did not want to believe that existing structures could not cope. He was adamant that intelligent economic management would bring an eventual end to the crisis. He proposed a one year moratorium on all international and government debt payments in the hope that this would enable Europe, also in the throes of financial collapse, to stabilize its finances. In December 1931 he proposed the creation of the Reconstruction Finance Corporation, a federally chartered and owned corporation which was authorized to lend funds to banks, railroads, building and loan associations, and insurance companies. The aim was quite simply to guarantee the survival of the institutions that were necessary to the maintenance of the economy. It succeeded in the sense that it shored up these vital businesses and prevented some from certain collapse. But it failed to revive the economy. Funds were not put in the hands of those out of work. There was no revival in demand and manufacturers had no incentive for increasing production.

The inability of the economy to shake off the slump put the country into a despondent and even ugly mood. President Hoover, for all his genuine concern and innovation – he was not indifferent, as his political opponents insisted – was held in virtual contempt by those who relied on soup kitchens for their daily sustenance. Business leaders, who had been praised for the prosperity of the 1920s, were now seen as disreputable perpetrators of want and hardship. A Senate investigation revealed that J. P.Morgan had paid no income tax in 1931 and 1932. Ivar Kreuger, the Swedish 'Match King' and an international financier, was found after his suicide in Paris to have cheated American investors of a quarter of a billion dollars. In March 1932 Samuel Insull's utility empire collapsed, leaving behind losses of nearly $700 million. Despair gave way to anger. Hunger marches began. Farmers used agricultural implements to prevent banks from carrying out foreclosures. 'Farm holidays', or strikes, enveloped the countryside. Farmers refused to sell their produce, set up road blocks to prevent farm products from reaching market and dumped perishable commodities such as milk into ditches. First World War veterans began to demand immediate payment of a cash bonus, originally promised for 1945. When Hoover expressed his adamant opposition to the veterans, the former servicemen organized a 'Bonus Expeditionary Force' to march on Washington to press their demands. By June 1932, about 15,000 bonus marchers had arrived in Washington and some occupied abandoned buildings, or 'Hoovervilles' as they were contemptuously named. The administration lost its nerve and ordered the army to clear the bonus marchers. Tanks, cavalry and armed infantrymen were used to herd them away. The very men who had fought for American victory and had created the conditions for the emergence of the United States as the wealthiest nation on earth were now driven from Washington, perhaps with the same arms they had borne for their country. It seemed that an era had ended in an act of repudiation.

There was not just loss of faith in government and the business community. The United States' international standing seemed to be in decline. If the United States had prospered more than anywhere else in the 1920s, it had also shown itself to be more vulnerable to the depression in the 1930s. The slump hurt the United States more than it hurt the other advanced economies. Its rate of unemployment was worse. World trade had collapsed, partly as a result of tariff wars which it had initiated. The collapse was catastrophic in the United States. Its share of world commerce was reduced. Its share of world manufacturing output fell from 43.3 per cent in 1929 to 31.8 per cent in 1932. For the other main powers the proportions remained roughly stable, with the exception of the Soviet Union which more than doubled its share in the same period. The ability of the Soviet communists to insulate themselves from economic catastrophe was read as a lesson by some critics. It seemed as if capitalism could no longer deliver. As a result of its declining economic position, the United States under Presidents Herbert Hoover and his successor, Franklin Roosevelt, became more inward-looking. Policy makers felt that the United States should concentrate on its economic problems and that it could not take a leading role in dealing with the emerging dictatorships as long as its economy was in disarray. Thus as the world headed for its second suicidal cataclysm in the twentieth century, the Unites States tried to stay on the sidelines. Capitalism and the American system of government had to be saved. That was the brief of the political agenda of the 1930s. How that brief was was executed and how it was subsequently resolved and developed will be the theme of this book.

Further reading

Lester V. Chandler, *America's Greatest Depression* (New York, 1970).

William E. Leuchtenburg, *The Perils of Prosperity, 1914–1932* (Chicago and London, 1958).

Martin L. Fausold, *The Presidency of Herbert C. Hoover* (Lawrence, KS, 1985).

John K. Galbraith, *The Great Crash* (Boston, 1955).

Studs Terkel, *Hard Times: An Oral History of the Great Depression* (London, 1970).

2

The New Deal, 1933–1940

The election of Franklin D. Roosevelt as President of the United States in November 1932 marked the beginning of a new epoch in the history of the American Republic. Not only did Roosevelt establish an electoral coalition which would ensure Democratic majorities at all levels of government below that of President for the next five decades, but in the eight years between Roosevelt's inauguration in March 1933 and the bombing of Pearl Harbor by the Japanese in December 1941, the nature of American government was transformed. First, a new public philosophy, which stressed the federal government's responsibility for promoting the economic and social welfare of the citizens of the United States, replaced a public philosophy which had stressed the individual's responsibility for his own welfare. Second, the relationship between the federal government and the state governments was fundamentally altered as an assertion of federal power reduced the autonomy of the individual states. Third, the position of the President within the federal government was enhanced. It was to the President and not to Congress that people increasingly turned for solutions to the problems facing American society.

That such a radical change in the American political system was about to occur had only been hinted at during the 1932 election campaign. In his acceptance speech at the Democratic Convention, Franklin D. Roosevelt urged the delegates: 'Let it be from now on the task of our Party to break foolish traditions... I pledge you, I pledge myself, to a new deal for the American people.' The party platform, however, differed little from that of the Republicans. Only one clause, which committed the Democratic Party to the principle of 'continuous responsibility of government for human welfare', gave any indication of what was to follow. Even this rather bland and non-specific commitment was played down during the campaign. Although Roosevelt occasionally spoke of the need for economic planning and government regulation, he tended to hide his progressivism behind attacks on his opponent. Like most candidates running against an incumbent President, Roosevelt preferred to speak out against government spending, unbalanced budgets and an expanded bureaucracy. In a speech given in Pittsburgh on the 19 October 1932 Roosevelt lambasted the Hoover Administration for running an alleged billion dollar a year deficit and promised that he would cut the cost of government by 25 per cent. Only towards the end of the speech did he add that: 'If starvation and dire need on the part of any of our citizens make necessary the appropriation of additional funds which would keep the budget out of balance, I shall not hesitate to tell the American people the full truth and ask them to authorize the expenditure of that additional amount'. Ironically it was left to President Hoover to defend deficit spending and experimental measures such as the Reconstruction Finance Corporation and the Federal Home Loan Bank Act (1932).

In what was more a vote of no confidence in President Hoover and the Republican Party than a vote of confidence in Franklin D. Roosevelt and the Democratic Party, the Republicans were swept from national office in the elections of 1932. Roosevelt won 22,815,539 votes compared to Hoover's 15,759,930, and captured forty-two states with 472 electoral votes while Hoover carried a mere six states with a total of 59 electoral votes. In the US Senate the Democrats gained thirteen seats to win control of the chamber for the first time since 1918. In the House of Representatives they gained ninety seats to consolidate the control of the chamber they had held since 1930. These election results signalled the end of the majority status which the Republicans had enjoyed since 1896. The electoral coalition of blue-collar workers, middle-class liberals, Roman Catholics, Jews, European ethnic groups and white southerners that Roosevelt managed to put together would ensure Democratic majorities at most levels of government below the presidency for nearly fifty years. It was certainly sufficient to gain Roosevelt's re-election in 1936, 1940 and 1944. Although his margins of victory declined slightly in the later elections, Roosevelt remained an extremely popular President right up to his death in 1945.

Of paramount importance to the success of President Roosevelt was the fact that the electoral coalition which he had assembled ensured Democratic majorities in both Houses of Congress throughout his Administration. With secure Democratic majorities in Congress, Roosevelt was able to enact a programme of reform and recovery. That programme, the New Deal, began on 9 March 1933 when Congress met in a special session called by President Roosevelt to deal with what appeared to be the imminent collapse of the American banking system. After passing the Emergency Banking Act (1933), which extended the federal government's control over the banking system, Congress remained in session until 16 June 1933 to deal with a wide variety of economic problems. During the 'Hundred Days' of this special session the President and Congress worked closely together to produce an unprecedented outpouring of legislation designed to mitigate the worst effects of the Great Depression. The Unemployment Relief Act (1933) created the Civilian Conservation Corps (CCC) to provide work for men between the ages of eighteen and twenty-five. By the end of 1941 more than two million young men had been employed by the CCC on projects such as reforestation, flood control and soil conservation. The Federal Emergency Relief Act (1933) appropriated $500 million and established the Federal Emergency Relief Administration (FERA) to assist the states and cities in caring for the unemployed. The National Industrial Recovery Act (1933) created both the National Recovery Administration (NRA) to prepare codes of fair competition, and the Public Works Administration (PWA) to supervise the construction of roads, schools, hospitals, dams, bridges and other public projects. Between 1933 and 1939 the PWA spent approximately $5 billion on nearly 35,000 construction projects, and employed more than 500,000 people. The NRA codes were designed to prevent bankruptcy through cut-throat competition. Participating companies were permitted to fix prices and standardize their products, provided that they recognised the right of their workers to form unions and ended employment abuses, such as child labour. The Agricultural Adjustment Act (1933) created the Agricultural Adjustment Administration (AAA) to control the production of crops such as wheat, cotton, corn, rice and tobacco. The Farm Credit Act (1933) set up the Farm Credit Administration (FCA) to provide loans to farmers for production and marketing with the aim of enabling farmers to refinance farm mortgages. By 1935 the FCA had helped refinance approximately 20 per cent of the farm mortgages in the United States. The Tennessee Valley Authority Act (1933) established the Tennessee Valley Authority (TVA), a public corporation designed to exploit the power resources of the Tennessee River.

Some indication of the enormous scope of the New Deal can be gathered from the type of measures passed during the 'Hundred Days'. Not only was relief provided for the unemployed, farmers and for business, but the TVA represented an attempt to develop a region covering parts of seven states. Although important, the legislation of the 'Hundred Days' represented only a fraction of the New Deal. In subsequent years further measures sought to provide additional relief, establish a framework for economic recovery, and introduce some social reforms. The National Housing Act (1934) created the Federal Housing Administration (FHA) to insure mortgages made for the building of new homes and the improvement of existing homes. By 1941 the federal government had insured $3.5 billion in mortgages. The Securities Exchange Act (1934) and the Banking Act (1935) strengthened the government's control of the stock exchange and the banking system. The Trade Agreements Act (1934) led to a gradual reduction of American tariff rates in a series of reciprocal agreements with other countries. The Emergency Relief Appropriation Act (1935) established the Works Progress Administration (WPA) to provide work relief by funding public projects. Between 1935 and 1943 the WPA spent approximately $11 billion on 1.5 million projects and provided temporary employment to roughly 8.5 million people. The National Labor Relations Act (1935) created the National Labor Relations Board (NLRB) and guaranteed the right of workers to bargain collectively. The Social Security Act (1935) provided for a comprehensive system of unemployment benefit and old age pensions. The Soil Conservation and Domestic Allotment Act (1936) and the Agricultural Adjustment Act (1938) expanded the policy of conserving natural resources and continued the attack on rural poverty.

It has long been common to cite measures such as the National Labor Relations Act (1935) and the Social Security Act (1935) as evidence of an important change in the nature of the New Deal. Such arguments suggest that whereas the measures of the First New Deal (1933-1934) were concerned primarily with relief and recovery, the focus of the legislation of the Second New Deal (1935-1938) was social reform. Although it would be unwise to make too much of this distinction - there were efforts aimed at relief within the Second New Deal - the National Labor Relations Act (1935) and the Social Security Act (1935) are important in illustrating one of the major themes of the entire New Deal. That theme is what the economist J. K. Galbraith called the 'concept of countervailing power'. Rather than attempting a large-scale redistribution of wealth, the New Deal sought to redistribute economic power. By making it easier for workers to form trade unions, for example, Roosevelt hoped to provide some counter to the overwhelming power of the employers. Even the Social Security Act (1935) was concerned more with providing security to the old and unemployed than with redistributing wealth. The object of many of the measures of the New Deal was to increase the economic power of a disadvantaged group so that it might better be able to deal with a more advantaged group. As stated during his 1932 campaign, one of Roosevelt's main concerns was for 'the forgotten man at the bottom of the economic pyramid'.

The question of whether there was any coherent ideology underpinning the collection of measures and 'alphabet agencies' which constituted the New Deal has been a source of considerable debate. Such debate is not surprising since the various measures often had different aims and drew their inspiration from a wide variety of sources. Some of the programmes suggested a mild form of fascism; others suggested a mild form of socialism. Some seemed to be derived from a Progressive tradition that dated back to the late nineteenth century; others seemed alien to American culture. Some seemed well planned; others seemed opportunistic. Moreover, criticism of the New Deal came from both the right and left. In 1934 the American Liberty League was founded by leading Democratic politicians such as Al Smith and John W. Davis with the aim of halting the encroachment of government on private enterprise. Other opposition came from figures such as Father Coughlin, Huey Long and Upton Sinclair. Father Coughlin, a radio priest, founded the National Union of Social Justice and eventually announced his support for fascism. Huey Long, an extremely powerful senator from Louisiana, founded the 'Share Our Wealth' organisation and advocated a massive redistribution of wealth. He would certainly have challenged Roosevelt for the Democratic nomination in 1936 had he not been assassinated in Baton Rouge in 1935. Upton Sinclair stood as the Democratic candidate for governor of California in 1934 and was also a supporter of radical tax reform. Apart from providing some insight into the intentions of President Roosevelt, such concerns about the ideological coherence of the New Deal are of little practical relevance. What is important is the extent to which the New Deal signalled a new role for the federal government in American life. Unlike the somewhat arcane debates regarding the intellectual origins of the New Deal, the change in public philosophy occasioned by this development was to have profound consequences for the way in which the political system as a whole operated.

Underpinning the various measures of the New Deal and providing the coherence sought by so many, was a belief in the efficacy and validity of federal or national action. In his First Inaugural Address, delivered on 4 March 1933, President Roosevelt seemed to repudiate the long-held American view that the actions of the government in Washington DC posed a threat to individual liberty. Opening with the words 'This is a day of national consecration' Roosevelt continued to emphasize the word nation throughout his speech. He stressed that the problem of the Great Depression was a national problem and that the country had to address itself 'to putting our own national house in order'. The first task was 'the establishment of a sound national economy' with the ultimate goal 'of a rounded and permanent national life'. These goals were to be met by action on a 'national scale' with a degree of 'national planning'. All in all, some form of the word nation is used sixteen times in the speech, appearing in fourteen of the twenty-seven paragraphs. No other term even nears this usage. Liberty, equality, or the individual are not mentioned at all, while the word democracy is used only once.

The 'nationalism' stressed by President Roosevelt was a call both for an increased centralization of power within the federal government, and for the nationalization of American politics. He argued not only that the federal government should take the lead in combating the effects of the Depression, but also that the people should turn to the government in Washington DC for help. In many respects this was a radical break from past practices, particularly for the Democratic Party. If there had been a centralizing party in the United States it had tended in the past to be the Republicans. It had been the Republican Party which had preserved the Union in the face of secession by the southern states in 1861, and had provided government assistance for the expansion of American industry in the late nineteenth century. The 'nationalism' of the Republican Party had, however, been limited. Although it believed that the federal government had a legitimate right to interfere in the economy to perfect the market, it did not believe that government had a right to supersede the market. The view that the federal government should somehow 'manage' the economy, in the way suggested by Franklin D. Roosevelt, was simply not entertained by Republicans.

In his First Inaugural Address President Roosevelt expressed his belief that the American Constitution was flexible enough to facilitate an increased role for the federal government without any 'loss of essential form'. He also 'hoped that the normal balance of Executive and legislative authority may be wholly adequate to meet the unprecedented task before us', but recognized that 'an unprecedented demand and need for undelayed action may call for temporary departure from that normal balance of public procedure'. Roosevelt was, for the most part, correct in his view that the Constitution would endure without any 'loss of essential form'. Most of the basic principles of the Constitution - republicanism, the Separation of Powers and the system of checks and balances - survived the New Deal. The only casualty was federalism as the relationship between the federal government and the state governments was changed beyond recognition by the New Deal's assertion of national power. On the other hand, Roosevelt's belief that any change in the relationship between the executive and the legislature would be temporary was clearly mistaken. The New Deal heralded a growth in the power and prestige of the presidency which has hitherto proved to be permanent.

The New Deal changed the nature of American federalism in four important ways. First, the relief programmes led to an increase in spending by the federal government. Between 1929 and 1939 expenditure by the federal government on domestic programmes rose from a mere 1.5 per cent of Gross National Product (GNP) to 8.1 per cent of GNP. During this same period spending by the state governments increased from 2 per cent of GNP to 4.1 per cent of GNP. In other words, by 1939 the federal government was spending more money on domestic programmes than the state governments. Second, the federal government often required the state governments to agree to specific regulations before they were awarded funds for relief. Through the regulations it attached to funds, the federal government gradually extended its power and control over the states. Third, some of the payments authorized by the programmes of the New Deal went not to the state but to individuals. Social security payments, for example, were paid directly to individuals. In such cases the effect was to minimize the role of the state governments in an important area of domestic life. Finally, Roosevelt's exhortation for the American people to view their difficulties as part of a national problem changed the public's perceptions about the proper function of the federal government. Increasingly they turned to Washington DC rather than to their state capitals for solutions to their problems.

Such fundamental changes in the structure of American federalism did not go unchallenged. The Supreme Court, in particular, was initially reluctant to sanction the view expressed by President Roosevelt that the Great Depression was a national problem requiring national action. On 27 May 1935, in the case *Schechter Poultry Corporation v. United States* (commonly known as the 'sick chicken' case), the Court unanimously ruled the National Industrial Recovery Act to be unconstitutional. The Justices believed that the Act's codes of fair competition, which regulated wages and employment practices in various industries, constituted an unjustifiable extension of federal power. Chief Justice Charles Hughes argued that if the Act was allowed to stand '... there would be virtually no limit to the Federal power, and for all practical purposes we should have a completely centralized government'. On 6 January 1936 the Court similarly ruled the Agricultural Adjustment Act to be unconstitutional in the case *United States v. Butler*. By a majority of six to three the Court decided that the Act infringed upon the rights reserved to the states by the tenth amendment to the Constitution. Justice Owen Roberts, writing the opinion for the majority, argued that:

> It does not help that local conditions throughout the nation have created a situation of national concern; for this is but to say that whenever there is a widespread similarity of local conditions, Congress may ignore constitutional limitations on its own powers and usurp those reserved to the states.

A clearer rejection of the nationalism of President Roosevelt would be difficult to imagine.

In the sixteen months between January 1935 and April 1936 the Supreme Court invalidated New Deal statutes in eight out of the ten cases it heard involving legislation sponsored by President Roosevelt. Such actions left the future of the New Deal very uncertain, and led Roosevelt to make what was arguably the biggest political mistake of his presidency. Buoyed by his landslide electoral victory in November 1936 the President determined to change the composition of the Court. Constitutionally unable to remove members of the federal judiciary, Roosevelt presented legislation to Congress on 5 February 1937 which provided that whenever a federal judge who had served ten years or more failed to retire after reaching the age of seventy, the President might appoint an additional judge to the court on which he served. No more than fifty new judges might be appointed and the maximum size of the Supreme Court was set at fifteen. Roosevelt sought to justify such legislation by suggesting that the efficiency of the federal judiciary would be improved by an influx of younger members. In reality it was an attempt to exert his power over what had hitherto been an uncooperative Supreme Court. No fewer than six of the nine members of the Court were over seventy, and by making six additional appointments Roosevelt would have been able to shape the Court in his own image.

Although Roosevelt had been careful to describe his plan as a reorganization of the federal judiciary, it soon came to be characterized as an attempt to 'pack' the Supreme Court. Many people viewed it as 'a naked bid for dictatorship' which sought to undermine the constitutional doctrine of the Separation of Powers. Not only had Roosevelt seriously mistaken the general mood of the public, but the 'court-packing' plan also weakened his political position. For the first time the Democratic coalition began to unravel at the edges as conservative southern Democrats voted with the Republicans to defeat the measure in the Senate. In his haste to deal with the Supreme Court Roosevelt had unwittingly provided the catalyst for the birth of the 'conservative coalition'. Never again would he be able to enjoy clear majorities in Congress.

Meanwhile the Court itself had acted to remove the need for any reform of the judicial system. Whether because of a recognition of the clear mandate given to the New Deal by the 1936 election results, or because of the threat to its independence posed by the 'court-packing' plan, the Supreme Court changed direction. In April 1937 Chief Justice Hughes and Justice Roberts voted with the progressive minority, Justices Stone, Cardoza and Brandeis, in the case *National Labor Relations Board v. Laughlin Steel Corporation*. By five votes to four the Court validated the National Labor Relations Act (1935). Over the next four years four of the most ardent opponents of the New Deal retired from the Court and were replaced by strong supporters of President Roosevelt. Together with the apparent changes in attitude of Hughes and Roberts, these alterations in the Court's composition brought about a *volte face* in the Court's approach to the role of the federal government in national economic life. After the *Laughlin* case, the Court upheld every New Deal statute which came before it. In *Stewart Machine Company v. Davis* (1937) it upheld the Social Security Act; in *Mulford v. Smith* (1939) it upheld the second Agricultural Adjustment Act and in *U.S. v. Darby* (1941) it upheld the Fair Labor Standards Act. By 1941 the Court had fully accepted the enlargement of the federal government's authority over economic matters. The federal government had established its right to operate in every sphere of the national economy. It could regulate wages, prices, employment and welfare. Furthermore, there would be no constitutional barrier to the adoption of Keynesian techniques for managing the economy when such ideas gained credence in the aftermath of the Second World War.

In addition to redefining the boundaries between the federal and state governments, the New Deal also brought about significant changes in the relationship between the President and Congress. The combination of a deep national crisis, new expectations about the function of the federal government, and President Roosevelt's long incumbency served to transform both the role and structure of the presidency. In less than a decade Roosevelt firmly established the principle that the President had a duty to initiate and seek support for legislative programmes rather than merely being expected to show an interest in the proceedings of Congress. He presided over an enormous growth in the amount of resources available to the White House. From a presidency with limited staff support there developed an extensive presidential bureaucracy. Finally, and perhaps most importantly, he propelled the presidency to the centre stage of American life. During his Administration the quantity and quality of public attention to the presidency increased dramatically as Roosevelt came to symbolize American government.

The transformation of the presidency began with Roosevelt's First Inaugural Address when he confidently announced that he would request war powers over the economy if Congress failed to act. Throughout the Address he stressed the leadership he would bring to the country, declaring that 'The people of the United States ... have asked for discipline and direction under leadership. They have made me the present instrument of their wishes. In the spirit of the gift I take it'. In short, right from the beginning of his Administration, Roosevelt sought to establish the presidency as the focus of the American people's hopes, fears and expectations. He came to personalize government. In his 'fireside chats' over the radio he would explain the actions of the government like a father talking to his family, and like most fathers would have to answer a myriad of questions. One White House aide noted that 'President Roosevelt was getting about as much mail a day as President Hoover received in a week. The mail started coming in by the truckload. They couldn't even get the envelopes open.' No longer did people turn to Congress to solve their problems. Instead they increasingly turned to the occupant of the White House for solutions to the ills of society.

One important consequence of the presidency's enhanced role in the national political life of the United States under Franklin D.

Roosevelt was a change in the structure of the presidential office. With more expected of the President the existing resources of the office were found to be insufficient. At first Roosevelt tried to overcome such problems in an informal manner by hiring a series of policy advisers who were officially on the payrolls of executive agencies outside the White House. Known collectively as the 'Brain Trust', advisers such as Raymond Moley, Adolph A. Berle and Rexford Tugwell were particularly influential in determining the direction of the early New Deal. Later important 'brain trusters' included Thomas Corcoran, Benjamin Cohen and Harry Hopkins. In time, however, it was felt that a more formal support structure was required. Just such a support structure was proposed in the 1937 report of the Committee on Administration of the Federal Government, commonly known as the Brownlow Committee. Arguing that the dramatic expansion in the responsibilities of the executive branch under Roosevelt meant that 'the President needs help', the Brownlow Committee recommended the establishment of an Executive Office of the President (EOP). After considerable political debate in Congress the EOP was finally created by the Executive Reorganisation Act (1939). The emergence of the modern presidency was now complete. Under Roosevelt the office had gained first a new role, and then a new structure. Future Presidents would find it difficult to escape from the legacy of Franklin D. Roosevelt.

So great was the transformation in American government brought about by the New Deal that Theodore Lowi, a distinguished political scientist, has characterized it as signalling the end of the First American Republic. Traditional American liberalism, with its emphasis upon the individual, was replaced by welfare, or interest group liberalism, in which different groups in society seek ever greater favours from the government. In short, through its emphasis on what the federal government could do to alleviate the problems of society, the New Deal created an environment for the proliferation of interest groups. Any group with a grievance would in future turn to Washington DC for support. Just how the federal government has balanced these ever increasing demands when faced with strictly limited resources would be an enduring theme of the next five decades of American history. In 1940, however, such problems remained for the most part in the future. The New Deal had provided relief for millions and helped promote an economic revival which, although leaving 14 per cent of the American workforce unemployed, gave the people of the United States a new confidence in their political institutions. The fact that the national debt of the United States doubled in the six years between 1933 and 1939 as the federal government struggled to cope with the financial consequences of its new found activism went largely unnoticed. In any case, such concerns would become irrelevant as the country armed itself for war.

Further reading

John M. Auswang, *The New Deal and American Politics: A Study in Political Change* (New York, 1978).

Anthony J. Badger, *The New Deal: The Depression Years, 1933-1940* (London, 1989).

Ellis W. Hawley, *The New Deal and the Problem of Monopoly* (Princeton, 1966).

William E. Leuchtenburg, *Franklin D.Roosevelt and the New Deal, 1932-1940* (New York, 1963).

Albert U. Romasco, *The Politics of Recovery: Roosevelt's New Deal* (New York, 1963).

3

The US and the Second World War, 1939-1945

As Americans watched the catastrophic chain of events that was to lead to the second world war in less than a quarter of a century, they drew lessons from their earlier entanglements. They remembered that back in 1914 their president, Woodrow Wilson, had repeatedly declared his intention to keep the United States out of war, but that he had been unable to fulfil his promise. Some believed that he had been manipulated into the war by the connivance of powerful interest groups. The majority of Americans felt that the United States had not been master of its own fate. Decisions had been made, in Europe's capitals and elsewhere, that had pushed the United States into a war it did not want. They were determined that this would not happen again.

All over the globe, militaristic powers and ambitious dictators were expanding their forces. In the Far East Japan marched into Manchuria and converted it into a puppet state. This was just a prelude to a full-scale war of conquest against China. In Germany, Adolf Hitler, who became Chancellor in 1933, called for the destruction of the treaty of Versailles and proclaimed that he intended to extend control over all German-speaking peoples. He began to arm. In 1936 his armed forces reoccupied the Rhineland in violation of the Versailles treaty. Two years later he forced the union between Germany and Austria and in the autumn of 1938 he took the Sudetenland from Czechoslovakia. Meanwhile the Italians, under Benito Mussolini, invaded Ethiopia in October 1935. And in 1936 the Spanish army revolted in Morocco and there began the long agony of the Spanish Civil War.

Most Americans were absorbed by the problems of the Great Depression and wanted to concentrate their resources on combating their economic difficulties. They hoped that problems overseas would remain distant – they did not want to become involved. They watched Britain, France and the western powers make concession after concession, and like them, hoped that such acquiescence would satisfy the ambitions of the militarists. They could not, however, rely on the restraint or diplomacy of the other great powers. They had to forestall the possibility of being dragged into another conflict. Accordingly, three Neutrality Acts were passed between 1935 and 1937. These laws were based on a particular interpretation of the events leading up to the United States' participation in the First World War. According to this version, businesses had dragged the United States into the war by making the nation dependent on the war trade. The legislation of the 1930s was designed so that the same mistakes would not be repeated.

The Neutrality laws required the President to embargo arms shipments, restrict loans to nations at war and to take no responsibility for travellers on belligerent ships. The laws were specifically designed to tie the President's hands and to restrict his initiative. But they also served, unwittingly, to aid aggression. Invariably it was the victim of aggression which needed strategic materials and capital. When Mussolini attacked Ethiopia in 1935, Roosevelt invoked the act but it made little difference to Ethiopia's fate. In the Far East the President was able to get round the laws, since neither Japan nor China had declared war. The United States carried on the war trade. Another Neutrality law passed in 1937 gave the President discretionary authority to furnish goods other than arms, provided the purchasers did not pay for them on credit, and they were taken away in ships carrying their own flag. In this way, the valuable war trade was preserved without incurring the military risk of having to defend it. Neutrality legislation may have salved the consciences of isolationists and assured those who distrusted presidential power, but it had no impact on world events. As the armies of Japan and Germany marched on to newer conquests and ultimate international conflagration, they took little account of the United States. There was little need – for the most part it stood by, apparently intent on keeping out of the fray.

The outbreak of war in September 1939 was to change things. Hitler's lightning victory in Poland was accompanied by the Soviet occupation of Eastern Poland, a manoeuvre to which the Germans had agreed under the terms of the Nazi–Soviet Pact. After the division of Poland, events began to move fast. In October the Baltic states of Latvia, Estonia and Lithuania agreed to permit Soviet troops onto their soil, a prelude to the incorporation of those countries the following year into the Soviet Union. In November the Soviets invaded Finland. In more distant theatres the Japanese completed their occupation of the most populous and productive areas of China.

The rapidity of these events and their far-reaching consequences forced Americans to assess their policies carefully. Their reactions were varied. Most of them experienced a sense of outrage. With only a few exceptions, Americans found German and Japanese hostilities morally distasteful and threatening to international stability. But there was still no consensus of what the United States could and should do to contain the fighting and to keep it away from its own shores. Americans knew one thing: they wanted to keep out of the war. The question was how. They could either adhere to a version of the Neutrality laws and keep their entanglements to a minimum, or they could use their enormous productive resources to deter potential aggressors and to assist those nations that were actively resisting them. Strict abidance by the Neutrality laws, with their cash and carry provisions, could directly serve to help aggression and to hinder the efforts of those nations with whom the United States shared sympathy and mutual interests. If Britain and France could not afford or were not permitted to buy vital American supplies then the United States would be abetting an Axis victory.

The President, Franklin Roosevelt, was well attuned to the vagaries and divisions in public sentiment. He knew that sudden changes in the development of the war could alter matters. But he could not be seen to move too fast in the taking of initiatives. At first he resisted pressures for substantial increases in national defence spending and rapid industrial mobilization. He leaned where he could and in stages. The President was aware that events were moving quickly and that Neutrality legislation did not accurately reflect the vicissitudes of opinion. 'This nation will remain a neutral nation,' he had proclaimed at the outbreak of war, 'but I cannot ask that every American remain neutral in thought as well. Even a neutral has a right to take account of facts. Even a neutral cannot be asked to close his mind or his conscience.' The President knew that public opinion responds to changing conditions. Americans would find it increasingly difficult to accept that a great power like the United States could not pursue its own interests abroad as a result of laws drawn up in different circumstances. It was simply a question of time. The United States possessed the ability to protect itself. But it would have to learn to identify its interests and to admit that it had the power to shift the balance in its favour.

As Hitler unleashed his military might, with stunning victories in Norway, Denmark, Holland, Belgium and France, America began to discover its slumbering power. Both Wilson and Roosevelt had learned that a democracy cannot exercise its full diplomatic potential if the public is not supportive. A double transformation took place in 1940. A market place developed for an alternative foreign policy, a policy that would acknowledge the fact that the nation could not achieve its objectives unless the full power of the state were used. At the same time the President recognized that the political mechanisms that would have to be activated to realize this change were sluggish. Germany had revolutionized the art of war, and its army was poised at the English Channel. Nothing seemed to get in Hitler's way. The sea and the potential might of the United States were the last barriers. Roosevelt did not mince matters. An Axis victory, he warned, 'would endanger the institutions of democracy in the Western World and ... the whole of our sympathies lies with those nations that are giving their life blood in combat against these forces'. The President had no doubt that the United States should endeavour to secure an Allied victory, with everything short of war. Public opinion shifted too. Congress voted a sum of two and a half billion dollars in under a month after the Wehrmacht's thrust into France and Belgium. By the end of the year it had voted for a fivefold increase in defence spending.

The second major change lay in the growth of executive power in the conduct of foreign policy. Roosevelt had familiarized himself with the fuller use of presidential power during the New Deal. In the 1930s he felt that he had been given a mandate for extending the presidential office as the only effective means of combating the economic depression. But in foreign affairs he had to tread carefully. Americans wanted peace and were not happy to give the President latitude. The most compelling characteristic of neutrality legislation was that **law** determined and defined the purposes of foreign policy. It was specifically designed to place a strait-jacket on presidential power. However, as the isolationist consensus began to crumble, Roosevelt realised that judicious use of executive power could serve the purpose of unleashing American resources to aid the beleaguered allies. Furthermore it would liberate the policy-making process from the scrutiny of Congress. The opportunity came when a faction of an interventionist pressure group, the Committee to Defend America by Aiding the Allies, suggested to Roosevelt that he could use his personal authority to dispose of government surpluses by transferring fifty over-age destroyers to England in exchange for bases on British possessions in the western hemisphere. Roosevelt embraced the plan enthusiastically. He argued that it represented a strategic gain for the United States and so did not contravene the Neutrality laws. His sense of confidence was further boosted when opinion polls showed overwhelming support for the deal. He could now boast that isolationism was a 'delusion', and that American military *matériel* played a formative role in the containment of Nazism.

The events that led to the United States' final participation in the war all had a common thread. As a non-belligerent, the United States became increasingly aware of its considerable ability to influence the solvency and survival of other nations. On 29 December, 1940, the President stated that it was the policy of the United States to keep the war away from the United States. But he stated that the most effective way was for the United States to become 'the great arsenal of democracy'. The nation's productive efforts would be geared towards helping Britain. 'Never before since Jamestown and Plymouth Rock has our American civilization been in such danger as now,' he proclaimed. These were not just rousing words. The United States now began the massive military and industrial mobilization which not only drew it closer to war but also to the status of a superpower. The most crucial development was the passage of the Lend–Lease act in 1941. Lend–Lease inextricably intertwined the nation's resources with Britain. It vested sweeping power in the president to procure any article for any country whose defence was deemed vital to American security. He could sell, transfer or exchange goods and make any arrangement for repayment that he saw fit. Lend–Lease established the United States as the prime producer of military supplies and prepared the nation for accepting that its economy was bound up with the security of the rest of the world. The nation geared itself to perform this new role. The Office of Production Management was set up to ease problems of supply, encourage the conversion of plant for the new requirements and to iron out labour disputes and other bottlenecks. Its successor, the War Production Board, created special inducements to business to fulfil contracts and to undertake new research and implement technology. 'If you are going to go to war ... in a capitalist country,' wrote Henry Stimson, Secretary of War, ' you have to let business make money out of the process or business won't work.' Thus another achievement of the defence crisis and later the war itself was the rehabilitation of big business. It regained the reputation it had lost after the crash of 1929 and its saviour was the very government that had initiated the New Deal. Business and the American public were now enlisted in the campaign to defeat Nazism.

The final blow to the United States' attempt to fight the war with its productive might rather than with the blood of its own men came not from Germany but from Japan. Since its advance on Manchuria in 1931, Japan had sought to carve out for itself a new empire in Asia. Its ambitions were fuelled by the dual stimuli of militarism and economic imperialism. It was dependent on raw materials from the United States and Southern Asia. If it could secure captive markets in Asia, it would be freed of that dependence. Japan sought, therefore, to expel the European powers from their colonial possessions and to subdue China, the largest prize of all. But the United States regarded the conquest of China as a threat. For one thing a radical change in Asia could undermine its own possessions and bases in the Pacific. The United States also recognized that China possessed enormous economic potential and that a Japanese hegemony would undermine the United States' ability to realize that potential. Matters did not end in China. After the German occupation of France and the Netherlands, there was nothing to stop the Japanese filling the vacuum left by the French and Dutch in their colonies in Indochina and the East Indies. Above all, if Japan completely conquered China, the entire land mass of Europe and Northern Asia would be under the dominion of one of the Axis powers. Thus the United States sought to challenge and check those Japanese designs. Again, the question was how.

The United States found itself in an awkward and absurd position. It was still exporting to Japan scrap iron and petroleum, products that were vital to Japan's military operations. It could place an embargo on these products; but that would force Tokyo to look elsewhere for supplies – and again the colonies of South East Asia were a tempting source. Alternatively the United States could appease Japan and make it dependent on the United States in the process. It decided to move cautiously by restricting trade on selected products. The Japanese were mindful of their dependence on American oil, and sought, through their ambassador in Washington, Admiral Kichisaburo Nomura, to reach an agreement. But they were unsuccessful. The United States insisted on a withdrawal from China, equality of commercial opportunity and an abandonment of Japan's New Order. The Japanese were unwilling to concede. Taking advantage of Hitler's surprise invasion of the Soviet Union in June 1941, it demanded the right to station troops in the whole of Indochina. The mood in Washington hardened. Japanese assets in the United States were frozen in July 1941 thus severing all trade. If Japan wanted oil it would have to look south to

Malaya and the Dutch East Indies. Tokyo knew this was likely to result in war. So the Japanese cabinet, under General Hideki Tojo, decided that a lightning pre-emptive strike against the United States' war-making capacity would reap advantage. After a last-ditch attempt at diplomacy failed, Japanese fighter-bombers set out for their fateful rendezvous in Pearl Harbor where the American Pacific fleet was stationed. In the crippling and relentless attack on American shipping, some 2,400 Americans lost their lives and fourteen heavy warships were disabled. The next day Roosevelt apppeared before Congress, dubbed that day as one 'that will live in infamy' and asked for a declaration of war. The isolationism and pacifism of sections of the American public seemed to evaporate instantly. Isolationist lobbies, including America First, disappeared without trace and America was finally involved in the Second World War. It marked not only the end of the struggle to keep the United States out of the imbroglio of world conflict, but also the beginning of the United States' role as the great player on the world stage.

The act that was to be played out for the next three and a half years was to have consequences that far transcended the fighting. From the very beginning of the war the United States began to address itself to the shape of the peace that was to come in its wake. It was a war that was fought with great self-confidence. The Americans never contemplated their own defeat. Even temporary military setbacks – and there were not many of those – were regarded with surprise. Their confidence was not without foundation. The economic resources of the United States were vast. The federal budget rose from about $9 billion in 1939 to $100 billion in 1945. In the same period the gross national product rose from $91 billion to $166 billion. New industrial products, like synthetic rubber, were introduced and increased mechanization revitalized old and tapped new industries. Full employment returned. Men and women now had money to spend again. Despite rationing and wage controls the shops were full with both goods and customers. A further boost to this sense of confidence was the conduct of the war itself. No bombs fell on the United States; no battlefields were located on American soil. The troops were well supplied. In the first year of the war military engagements were confined largely to the Pacific theatre. All this seemed a far cry from London's blitz or the starvation experienced in Moscow and Leningrad.

Although America mobilized for war in an environment of plenty, its experience of mobilization was not without its trials. Over fifteen million men and women felt the wrench of parting as they went off to serve in the armed forces. Those who did not flocked to enjoy the new employment opportunities. There were labour shortages in the ship-yards and aircraft factories. As is so often the case in war, sex roles changed dramatically. By 1945 over six milliom women had entered the workforce, an increase of over 50 per cent. In aircraft plants about 40 per cent of the workers were female. Married women left their homes to go out to work; if there had been a stigma to women's work, it was disappearing. Blacks too began to participate more fully, though they still suffered discrimination. About one million served in the armed forces, and in almost every theatre of war. But they usually served in segregated units. About two million blacks were working in war plants by the end of 1944, though they often had the most menial jobs and lower pay. After a threatened march on Washington in 1941, the President established a Fair Employment Practices Committee whose task was to enforce a presidential directive forbidding discrimination in defence work and training programmes. While it was not that effective, it did recognize the crucial role performed by blacks in the national economy. As blacks left rural areas of the South to serve in the armed forces or work in defence industries, they also became more aware of their electoral power. Nevertheless, African Americans probably had more opportunities than the 100,000 Americans of Japanese descent who were forcibly removed from their homes on the West Coast to relocation camps in the interior. They were just hapless victims of fear and racial prejudice, caught in the whirlwind of anti-Japanese hysteria after the attack on Pearl Harbor.

For the administration, the problems of ethnic minorities were little more than awkward sideshows. The economic boom, combined with the fact that the war was not fought on American soil, gave the United States one very special advantage in its planning for warfare, namely time. The military planners had two main tasks. The first was to develop a military strategy that would bring the war to a rapid conclusion while minimizing the loss of American lives. The second was to establish its war aims so that it could synchronize its military strategy, its foreign economic policy and its diplomatic posture towards those ends. The basis of its military strategy was simple. Despite Pearl Harbor it regarded Germany as the principal threat. The United States believed that Japan was overextended and that its limited resources and the strain on its navy would eventually cause the Japanese empire to crumble. Germany posed the greater threat, at least in President

Roosevelt's judgement. Germany occupied most of Europe, had a formidable presence in North Africa and had penetrated deep into Soviet territory. Britain and the Soviet Union would have to be sustained at all costs. If they were to surrender or make a separate peace the United States would stand alone against Germany and Japan. Furthermore, despite the United States' poor record in admitting Jewish refugees from Germany, there was a profound revulsion at the rule of murderous thuggery in Nazi Europe. Thus Roosevelt's prime aim was to knock out Germany and to create a world order that eliminated all vestiges of Nazism and made its reappearance impossible.

The Soviets also wanted to see Germany vanquished. The appalling casualties suffered on the Eastern Front left the Soviets, under the iron-fisted rule of Josef Stalin, in no doubt as to how this should be achieved. At the end of 1941, when the United States entered the war, the might of the Wehrmacht was concentrated in the Soviet Union. The Soviets desperately wished to divide the German army in two, so that its force would be deflected. That could easily be done, the Soviets maintained, by a massive landing of British and American troops along the French coast. Such a second front would force Hitler to divert some of his troops from the beleaguered Soviet Union. The Americans agreed, at least in principle. But it was not an easy task. Unlike the Soviets, who were fighting for their very existence, the Americans had the option of timing such an invasion and of considering alternatives. They faced other pressures. Winston Churchill, the Prime Minister of Great Britain, did not want to risk a landing in France, at least not straight away. He believed that the Atlantic allies should land in North Africa, and hold down German troops there. A landing in North Africa would become the springboard for an invasion of Southern Europe, either through Italy or, possibly, the Balkans. This was, in Churchill's view, more feasible. It would encounter less furious resistance from the Germans, would restore French authority in North Africa, and pre-empt any Soviet penetration of the Balkans. Above all, it would not require so much military hardware and would expose allied troops to fewer risks. The British had their way. Allied landings (Operation TORCH) took place in November 1942 and killed the momentum for an invasion of France, which would not now take place until June 1944.

The decision to delay a second front in Western Europe had long-term consequences. The Soviets chose to interpret that delay as a sign of bad faith. The President, they rightly pointed out, had pledged an early attack in December 1941 and had reneged. The change of mind had enabled the Germans to inflict further casualties and devastate entire communities. It was, they maintained, supposed to be an **allied** war effort; their western partners cared only for their own short-term safety. The Americans felt slighted by these allegations. Their reasons for the postponement of the Second Front were, they countered, impeccable. Military campaigns could only be undertaken if armies were sufficiently trained and equipped. They were not ready. They maintained they were sensitive to the Soviets' plight. A massive quantity of supplies through the Lend–Lease programme was still sent to the Soviets, often at great risk to allied shipping. Germans were still being heavily engaged. The amphibious operations in North Africa were a formidable substitute; the aerial bombing campaigns were severely hindering the German war effort. Furthermore, American efforts in the Pacific held the Japanese down and removed the danger of a new front against the Soviet Union in the East.

The war aims of the United States were closely tied to its military strategy. The Americans wanted the peace to prevent future wars. The lessons of the past had to be learned. The principal lesson, they believed, was the necessity for more assertiveness about their goals in international relations and for recognition that their national interest could not be divorced from the structure of the governments and economies of other nations. The international order had collapsed in the 1930s because nations had not subscribed to a common code of political conduct. Americans believed that the individualist values of a liberal society were indispensable to a peaceful and prosperous order. These values would be realized, almost by some magical process, if all nations were allowed to settle their own futures. This commitment to self-determination was not substantially different to Woodrow Wilson's blueprint after the First World War. But this time the United States had to find a means of guaranteeing the new order.

Prosperity, Americans claimed, was the key to international harmony. The Secretary of State, Cordell Hull, was perhaps the most persistent exponent of this view. According to Hull, the best means of achieving such prosperity was through the liberalization of trade and investment opportunity. He wrote in his memoirs that 'if we could get a freer flow of trade ... so that one country would not be deadly jealous of another and the living standards of all countries might rise, thereby eliminating the economic dissatisfaction that breeds war, we might have a reasonable chance of lasting peace'. The proponents of free trade also believed that the steady flow of goods would draw societies closer together by virtue of their contact with and dependence on those goods. But it was not just the political effects of an open door that were emphasized, though their importance should not be underestimated. Flourishing postwar trade and investment would maintain the American economy at its wartime strength and provide markets for the vast volume of goods that the reconverted industries would produce. Humanitarianism and self-interest were inextricably intertwined. Finally, the United States hoped that institutional co-operation after the war would promote these common goals. A successor to the League of Nations would have to be created to oversee the peace. The new collective security organization would be overseen by the superpowers, the United States, the Soviet Union, Britain and, rather oddly, China. The new international agency would perform peacekeeping functions and be empowered to enforce the peace with sanctions. The United States could no longer depend on suasion and independent action. It would have to promote the new order actively.

The United States' ideas for international harmony did not coincide with those of the Soviets. Indeed they were incompatible. This incompatibility produced not only wartime acrimony but would mould the shape of the postwar settlement and the Cold War that came in its wake. The Soviets were hardly likely to warm to American liberalism. The Soviets had no illusions about the primacy of the national interest. The United States' cautious military strategy was the obvious testament to that. A liberal order was not the basis of Soviet society. Roosevelt's vaunted 'four freedoms', with their emphasis on libertarianism, were alien and indeed threatening to the apparatus of state under Stalin. Even more important, the Soviets' war aims were overwhelmingly preoccupied with the provision of security along the borders of the Soviet Union. Stalin made it quite clear what he wanted. After the war there were cries of bad faith, but by and large the Soviets broke faith only on their methods of implementation. They did not disguise their territorial and political goals for Eastern Europe. Stalin, no less than Roosevelt, wanted peace and harmony. He was not prepared, however, to rely on the capitalist West for the provision of that security. He was content to see the establishment of a United Nations and to see self-determination in certain countries. But not on the Soviet Union's own borders. And particularly not in Poland, where the hostilities had begun in 1939.

Stalin believed that he could guarantee Soviet security in Eastern Europe by two methods. First, the frontiers of Poland would have to be changed in order to enlarge the Soviet Union. Eastern Poland had been assigned to the Soviets under the Hitler–Stalin pact of 1939. The Soviets had no intention of surrendering it. New frontiers would provide the Soviets with more easily defensible territory. Poland would receive compensation for lost land in the West by detaching part of Germany and assigning it to Poland. Second, Stalin was insistent that the governments of neighbouring nations would have to be friendly to the Soviet Union. Stalin knew that if the Americans had their way, and free elections were held in Poland and the other nations of Eastern Europe, unfriendly governments would be returned to office. He would use military power to secure sympathetic regimes. Such sympathetic governments would provide a protective shield against any future military attack from the West, particularly from Germany. They would also, though Stalin never specifically admitted it, provide the basis for the economic reconstruction of the Soviet Union.

Stalin's policies towards Poland placed American policy makers in a quandary. They wanted peace with the Soviets, but not at any price. Soviet war aims directly conflicted with those of the United States. Roosevelt had reaffirmed time and again his adherence to the principles of the Atlantic Charter, a declaration of principles drawn up jointly with the British in August 1941. The Charter had affirmed the principle of self-determination for all liberated nations. Roosevelt took these lofty objectives more seriously than Churchill. He did not have the compromising complication of an impatient empire. He also had to mirror the views of the electorate which was being mobilized to support a foreign policy that broke with tradition. Poland itself was an emotive issue. There were about six million Polish–Americans who formed an effective lobby. Their cause was aided by a growing sense of unease about the nature of the Soviet system and the regime that was likely to emerge in Poland in the wake of the Red Army's military advances. Two circumstances in particular contributed to these cooling appraisals of Soviet policy. In April 1943 a mass grave containing the corpses of several thousand Polish officers who had gone missing during the Soviet occupation of Poland was unearthed by the retreating Germans. Despite fierce denials and some puzzling inconsistencies of evidence, the finger of responsibility pointed to the Soviets. A year later in August 1944 the Soviets declined to come to the aid of the Polish Home Army which rose against their German masters in Warsaw. While the Soviet Union's refusal to move its forces which were amassed just outside the city had some justification – their troops were exhausted, overstretched, and not ready for hand-to-hand fighting in a city – the tone of their refusal and the consequences of their inaction shocked leaders in the United States. The Polish insurrectionists were dismissed as mere 'power-seeking criminals' by Stalin. He did not want to liberate Warsaw from the Nazis only to find it in the hands of bourgeois Poles who were aligned with the Americans and British. A quarter of a million Poles perished in the rebellion and an ancient city was reduced to rubble while the world looked on.

The United States found itself opposing Soviet policy in a number of theatres. That opposition was to become apparent in the wartime conferences that took place between the three powers. They met three times: in Teheran in November 1943, at Yalta in February 1945 and at Potsdam, just outside Berlin, in July 1945. While agreements on various issues including the most divisive ones were reached, they were little more than statements of intent. The powers needed a semblance of unity to maintain the momentum of fighting. They also hoped that the cooperation could be continued after the war. But the discussions revealed fundamental differences over the specific futures of Eastern Europe, Germany, and the Far East, and about the nature and conduct of international affairs.

About Germany, for example, the United States had no clear policy. They had called for the 'unconditional surrender' of the Germans and had made it clear that Germany would be subject to the dictates of the victorious powers. There were plenty of ideas, some of them half-baked, concerning the occupation and reconstruction of the Reich. But the United States had not developed any systematic, coherent plans. The State Department tended to take the wider view, seeing Germany as one component of the larger problem of the world's reconstruction. It believed that dismemberment would sow new seeds of resentment in the German population and would anyway invite a scramble for spheres of influence among the major powers. Similarly, harsh reparations and the destruction of the industrial capacity of the Germans would create unnecessary hardship and would require permanent policing, a prospect the United States did not relish. Above all, it looked forward to the creation of a new world economy, modelled on the principles of the Atlantic Charter. A postwar Germany that was unable to exploit its skills and resources would be wasteful and, in the last analysis, a drain on the United States' stretched resources. The State Department was not the only agency of government to consider the future of Germany. Henry Morgenthau, Secretary of the Treasury, had the President's ear for a short while. He was deeply moved by the excesses of Nazism and believed that a harsh peace was just and expedient. He advocated the destruction of Germany's war-making capacity and its reduction to a pastoral economy. This would accomplish a number of purposes at once. It would satisfy the desire for retribution, it would make the Soviets less fearful of a German revival, and would provide opportunities for the British and the Americans to fill those markets previously enjoyed by Germany. For a short while the Morgenthau Plan, as it came to be called, held sway. In September 1944 Morgenthau accompanied President Roosevelt to Quebec, where he presented the plan to Winston Churchill. When American troops began their occupation of Germany, they were ordered to undertake an extensive denazification programme and to limit German industrial production to the population's most rudimentary needs.

These confused, or to be more precise, divergent ideas were reflected in the wartime conference decisions. The United States' determined that it would play a formative role in postwar reconstruction but had not developed a working mechanism. It wanted rapprochement with the Soviet Union, but was not sure how this squared with its own democratic liberalism. Thus at Yalta Roosevelt agreed to a provisional figure of $20 billion in reparations, but made it clear he would want revisions later. Similar straddling occurred over Eastern Europe. Roosevelt knew that the Soviets were unlikely to alter their demands for territorial adjustments and pro-Soviet governments in Poland and other neighbouring countries. He agreed that the pro-communist Lublin government would form the nucleus of a reorganized postwar government in Poland. Just how such a reorganization would take place was never clear. At Yalta the issue of Poland was shelved. The President hoped that time and future events would somehow resolve the matter. He needed to confirm the United States' commitment to a liberal world order and to convince American public opinion that the United States would stand by its principles. Stalin helped Roosevelt keep up the pretence by agreeing to sign the Declaration on Liberated Europe, which called for the 'earliest possible establishment through free elections' of representative governments in the liberated nations of Europe. The Declaration was the means by which the United States would justify keeping a foot in the door of Eastern Europe.

As it happened the United States found that its greatest prospect for influencing the course of events was in the Far East. Until 8 August,

1945, when the Soviet Union declared war on Japan and entered Manchuria, the Red Army had no presence in the Far East. The United States enjoyed almost free rein. The theatre in China, the Pacific Islands and India remained an Anglo-American affair. It was understood that the occupation of Japan would be exclusively an American responsibility. The United States saw that a unique opportunity presented itself. In China the civil war between the communists under Mao and the Kuomintang under Chiang-Kai-shek had served to weaken the government. The United States was eager to restore stability and realised that a premium would be placed on a successful resolution of that conflict. Earlier in the war, Roosevelt had appointed General Joseph Stilwell to prepare Chinese forces for combat against the Japanese and had hoped that the modernization of the army would equip the Nationalists for the role of predominant power in postwar Asia. If China remained weak, the whole area would become unstable, particularly as a result of the unrest in the European colonies resulting from the Japanese occupation. The future was uncertain. The United States was determined to ensure that it could make an imprint on developments there. The President distanced himself from European colonialism and advocated a system of international trusteeship for selected colonies and mandated territories, such as Indochina and Korea. American enthusiasm (which would wane in the postwar years) for the restructuring of power was based on its desire to appear consistent with the principles of the Atlantic Charter and to establish the solidity of its credentials as the leader of liberal democracy. It was aware that the war had discredited European imperialism. If it presented itself as the architect and guardian of the new order, the United States could become the predominant power in the Far East. The raw materials and the opportunity for strategic footholds seemed to beckon. If the United States did not wield influence the Soviets would.

Indeed it was in the Far East that the final drama of the war was enacted, a drama that would establish the United States as the dominant military power of the postwar world. On 6 August, 1945, an atomic bomb was dropped on the Japanese city of Hiroshima and another bomb on Nagasaki, three days later. The effects of these two devices were devastating. About 110,000 people were killed and further tens of thousands injured. The bomb illustrated that modern warfare had taken a quantum leap forward. The United States now possessed the power to inflict mass destruction. That weapon alone had persuaded the warrior Japanese to bow to the inevitable and surrender.

The new president, Harry S. Truman, professed to being elated by the bomb. It promised untold new power for the United States, which now possessed a weapon that could almost guarantee a military victory. Furthermore its successful detonation had implications beyond the theatre of war. It would be a sobering deterrent to potential enemies of the United States. Until another power, particularly the Soviet Union, came to have atomic weapons, the United States could, if it so chose, reinforce its diplomacy with implied threats. Henry Stimson, Secretary of War, had advised Truman shortly before the dropping of the bomb that its influence would be 'decisive'. Foreseeing the new power of the bomb he predicted that 'we shall probably hold more cards in our hands later than now.' The Soviet Union would have to think twice before taking unilateral action. He even hoped that the bomb could be used as an inducement rather than a threat. 'The problem,' Stimson said, 'of our satisfactory relations with Russia [is] not merely connected with but [is] virtually dominated by the problem of the atomic bomb.' The bomb drastically altered the balance of power. Even if the United States could not impose its will, it possessed the confidence that can go with a sense of invincibility. Americans only had to look at their victorious allies to boost that confidence. Britain's financial resources were at straining point and the backbone of its power, the Empire, was seeking to break the bonds. The Soviet Union had lost over twenty million people; its fields were scorched; its industry was shattered and scattered, and its lesser allies in occupied Europe were waking up from their nightmare of deportations, summary mass murder, and vanished communities. The United States, in contrast, had known no occupation, no bombs, no disintegrating empires, no international debts and no serious consumer shortages. That sense of privilege and confidence was to have a profound effect on its dealings with the Soviet Union and on its own conception of self.

Further reading

John M. Blum, *V Was for Victory: Politics and American Culture During World War II* (New York, 1976).

Robert Dallek, *Franklin D. Roosevelt and American Foreign Policy, 1932-1945* (New York, 1979).

Robert A. Divine, *The Illusion of Neutrality* (Chicago, 1962).

Robert A. Divine, *Roosevelt and World War II* (Baltimore, 1969).

Gabriel Kolko, *The Politics of War: The World and United States Foreign Policy, 1943-1945* (New York 1968).

Frederick W. Marks, *Wind Over Sand: The Diplomacy of Franklin Roosevelt* (Athens, GA, 1988).

Vojtech Mastny, *Russia's Road to Cold War: Diplomacy, Warfare and the Politics of Communism, 1941-1945* (New York 1979).

Gaddis Smith, *American Diplomacy during the Second World War, 1941-1945* (New York, 1965).

4

The politics of reconversion, 1945-1952

The successful conclusion of the Second World War paradoxically served to highlight the conundrum of being a great power. The Axis armies had surrendered. The United States now faced the awesome task of preparing itself for the responsibilities of power and for ensuring that it possessed an economic infrastructure that would support this new role. In domestic politics the war had been an interlude rather than a watershed. Hostilities had come about in the midst of the worst economic depression the United States had ever faced. When the war was over the nation had to determine whether the measures of the New Deal, originally undertaken as an emergency device, should now be permanently enshrined in the nation's law books. Fears were rife that the termination of hostilities would unveil again an economic slump. All Americans were anxious to avoid the dislocations that had occurred after the end of the First World War. They wanted to avoid unemployment and to ease the transition to a peacetime economy. But they could not agree on the method of achieving these goals. The government possessed the power and the means to direct economic and social affairs as never before. The question was whether it should employ that power.

Until 1945 industry had concentrated on the production of war materials. That production now had to be reconverted to peacetime use. The soldiers returning from the battle-fronts would want either work or the education they had missed in order to go and fight. Markets had to be created for new products and for durables that had not been made in sufficient quantity during the war. If such markets could not be found and the demand for labour slackened, the federal government would have to decide whether to intervene again on the scale it did during the New Deal. Americans had accepted economic restrictions for the duration of the war. Prices had been controlled by the Office of Price Administration, rationing had been imposed on a variety of products and labour had made a 'no strike' pledge shortly after Pearl Harbor. Now the war was over they wanted a return to an unrestricted peacetime economy. Labour felt it had made sacrifices in a labour market where there was short supply; consumers wanted to spend their hard-earned savings. A planned economy would frustrate. However, a rapid growth in purchasing power would fuel inflation, and only tough economic controls would curb it. The question was, therefore, should government channel the process of reconversion, or should it only intervene in monetary matters when things began to bite?

The new President, Harry Truman, had been elevated to the office through force of circumstance, the untimely death of Roosevelt. He had not been regarded as an obvious successor. Rather he had secured the nomination as Vice-President because the two most prominent contenders for the post were unacceptable to powerful elements within the Democratic party. Truman had the fortune of having fewer enemies. Truman's concept of office was shaped by his own personal experiences and his reading of history (which he undertook with great appetite). He was genuinely awed by his rapid political elevation, but coped with that awe not through humility, although he was quite capable of it, but through an outward aura of confident command. He believed that he reflected the tastes and aspirations of ordinary Americans and so adopted a political style that was pugnacious and, on the surface, unquestioning. He showed little remorse over the bombing of Hiroshima and was dismissive of his Republican and anti-New Deal opponents. Indeed his presidency cannot be understood without an appreciation of his partisanship. For example, his contempt for the excesses of the anti-communist crusade was informed as much by his relentless commitment to the party as by moral repugnance. But it was not just party that moved him. He understood that the United States was now the most powerful nation on earth and the new President had every intention of preserving that power and hopefully extending it.

In the years after 1945 the United States had to adjust to its new status as a world power. In foreign affairs it would strive to become the spiritual leader of the western world and to buttress that role with unprecedented military and economic commitments abroad. At home it sought to develop a political culture that could assimilate this new status. It was an accommodation that was not easily made and one that consumed considerable political and intellectual energy. The adjustment was complicated by the social impact of the war. The war had raised expectations. Many Americans believed that the economic boom had passed them by. It was always others who seemed to profit. Blacks, for example, had made some economic advance, but still found themselves excluded from various jobs by unions and employers alike. In the South they still confronted legal segregation and pervasive disfranchisement. Labour felt it had not shared in the large profits made by manufacturing industry. The poor were still badly housed and restricted in their access to good health care. These groups wanted the federal government to extend the agenda of reform. On the other hand, a sizeable proportion of the population believed that social reform had gone far enough and that the tide should be stopped or even turned back. Republicans looked forward to tax reductions and the restoration of a market economy. They wanted the federal government to retrench and to abdicate from assuming responsibility for a wide spectrum of social welfare. Southern Democrats were wary of the voting power of blacks in the urban areas of the North and rued the fact that racial matters were increasingly a matter of political debate. In short, the debate that engaged Americans in the aftermath of war was not simply about the mechanics of reconversion but rather about the kind of political system that would govern for the next generation.

The most immediate concern was the matter of employment. In the first ten days of peace nearly two million people lost their jobs and 640,000 claimed unemployment compensation. The fear of depression gripped American workers. The administration thus saw that its first brief was to preserve employment and to control inflation – though a return to slump conditions would have effectively controlled inflation anyway. It pinned its main hope on the Full Employment Bill, which had been introduced in the Senate in January 1945. This Bill declared employment to be a right and required the government to ensure that sufficient jobs were available. The President was required to submit a 'national production and employment budget' each year. If he believed that there would be a shortfall in available jobs he was to draw up a programme for stimulating the economy. The President supported the Bill and reinforced it with measures of his own, including increased unemployment compensation, a new minimum wage law, permanent farm price supports and a public works programme. Congress passed an Employment Act, but not the version Truman wanted. It did not make federal spending to create jobs mandatory and relied on targets rather than express measures. Nevertheless, the Act declared it to be government policy to use 'all practical means' to create 'maximum employment'. A Council of Economic Advisers was established to report directly to the President on means of implementing these goals. The Employment Act was a recognition that economic planning and projections were legitimate governmental functions. Keynesianism had now fully captured the imagination of New Deal liberals and was to have an indelible stamp on monetary and fiscal policy.

The New Deal had not only created a revolution in government. It had also stimulated a special confidence in those groups which had comprised the Roosevelt coalition. Organized labour in particular was concerned to consolidate the gains it had achieved in the 1930s. It looked to government to protect the rights won under the National Labour Relations Act and other New Deal measures. It also sought to share the fruits of postwar prosperity. The unions believed that soaring corporate profits during the war had been made at the expense of labour. They were determined to restore or increase the purchasing power of their members and embarked upon an improvised programme of industrial action. There were stoppages in the steel, automobile and petroleum industries. Truman called a special Labour–Management Conference on 5 November, 1945 to try and smooth over differences but it only highlighted them. Management was convinced it could resist union demands and the unions were convinced that they now had the power to secure wage hikes. The conference ended without agreement. Problems could only be resolved by drawn-out bargaining procedures. Labour felt confident, though without much foundation. Its efforts in the war, it believed, and its position within the Democratic party warranted a militant campaign to obtain concessions on pay and working conditions. In April 1946 John L. Lewis's United Mine Workers struck for pay increases. In the following month the railroads were hit by strikes when the Railway Trainmen and the Locomotive Engineers refused to accept the government guidelines of an 18.5 cents an hour increase. The President seized the railroads and declared the strike to be one against the government. In an unexpected bombshell he announced to Congress that he would conscript the railroad workers and have the army run the railroads. He called for legislation that would restrict the right to strike against the government and would impose severe penalties on violators. He did not have to implement his threat to induct the strikers because the strike was called off with theatrical timing while he was still speaking. But the incident revealed two important developments. First, labour–management relations continued to be regarded as a legitimate area for intervention by the federal government. Second, labour could not count on the Democratic President for automatic sympathy and support. There was no clear postwar settlement in the area of industrial relations.

The role and power of organized labour was to be hotly debated in the early years of the Truman administration. The unions wanted to consolidate the gains they had made in the 1930s and enhance their power of collective bargaining. Those gains, however, were under threat as a result of the relaxation of controls on corporations and the general revolt within conservative ranks against the growth of governmental authority. This revolt was reflected in the mid-term elections of 1946, which had resulted in the election of a Republican majority to both houses of Congress, the first time Republicans had won such control since 1928. Republicans read the elections as a mandate for the revision of major New Deal reforms. Their principal target was the labour unions. The industrial turbulence during reconversion was blamed on the unions, which, conservatives believed, had grown too powerful. Congress was determined to impose curbs on them. In 1947 it passed the Taft–Hartley Bill, named after its two sponsors. The bill brought unfair labour practices as well as unfair management practices under legal jurisdiction. Although the bill placed more restrictions on labour, its basic rights were not seriously impaired. Under the terms of the bill, unions became liable for violations of contracts and they were forbidden to insist that individual employees must join a union as a condition of employment. Compulsory 'cooling off' periods were made mandatory in instances where the President declared a national emergency and initiated a federal court injunction. Other procedures for industrial disputes were imposed, although the fundamental framework of the National Labour Relations Act remained intact.

The legislation unleashed a storm of controversy. New Dealer and anti-New Dealer lobbied the White House furiously. Truman was placed on the horns of a dilemma. If he signed the bill, his standing with labour would have been destroyed and he would have generated a new nervousness about the future of the welfare state. If he vetoed, he would have redeemed much of the mistrust he had generated in his earlier dealings with labour and Democratic liberals. Truman calculated that the disaffection of Republicans and even some conservative Democrats was irreversible. He returned the bill with a stinging veto, though to no avail as Congress passed it over his objections. His refusal to sign did more to establish him as the heir to the New Deal than any other single act of his administration. The veto showed that for the time being the President would not reverse the political developments of the past decade and a half, and it assured the continuing political involvement of labour in the Democratic party.

Truman presided over an America whose confidence had been boosted by victory. He genuinely believed that the United States was the world's best hope for peace and prosperity. But that hope could only be realized if the United States developed a political and social system that was just, harmonious and exemplary to the rest of the world. He would not turn back the political clock. He would preserve and even extend the scope of the protective legislation of the 1930s. Thus he wanted no restrictions on the labour unions, proposed laws providing for the provision of health care, advocated federal subsidies to higher education and called for the provision of low cost housing. But the most sweeping proposals came in an area that was to occupy the political agenda for the next twenty years, namely civil rights.

American blacks still lived under the patterns of racial discrimination that had emerged in the United States in the years following the Civil War. In the South, blacks were still legally segregated in nearly every walk of life. African Americans attended separate schools and universities, were barred from 'white' hotels and bars, were buried in separate cemeteries and were segregated on the trains and buses. They were denied any meaningful access to the political process. A variety of laws prevented them from voting. Southern states had poll taxes which made it too expensive and too dangerous for blacks to vote. Despite a Supreme Court ruling in 1944, Southern states held primaries that were effectively open only to white members of the Democratic party. In the army blacks were segregated; in the nation's capital, which was then governed by Congress, segregation was almost universal. In the North, blacks could vote but they generally held the most menial jobs and were effectively barred from high quality housing. The war had made American blacks aware of their plight. Condemnations of the Nazis' racism seemed hollow when the United States harboured racial discrimination at home. The criticisms of Soviet society which were at the heart of the Cold War campaign could always be thrown back at the United States. Why was the barring of non-communist parties in Eastern Europe any different or any worse than the prevention of Negro voting in the South? Blacks realized that the time was now ripe to begin a concerted onslaught against the barriers to equality.

They were reinforced in their determination by the political power they were able to exert as a result of their growing electoral importance in the cities of the North. If the Democratic coalition was to be maintained, the administration could not afford to ignore their lobbying and campaigning.

Blacks were helped in their campaigns to ease racial discrimination by the folly of racists and the foresight of the Truman Administration. The President combined his own sense of decency with a keen political astuteness. Various civil rights organizations, including the National Association for the Advancement of Coloured People (NAACP), lobbied the administration and took test cases to court to remove the barriers faced by blacks. After a number of highly publicized acts of wanton and gruesome violence, the President appointed in December 1946 a Committee on Civil Rights to recommend measures that would safeguard rights and promote greater justice. In the following October the committee presented its report, *To Secure These Rights*. This report recommended a variety of measures to achieve freedom and equality. It proposed strengthening the legal machinery for protecting civil rights. Lynching was to be made a federal crime and the poll tax was to be outlawed. It called for the enactment of a Fair Employment Practices Bill and recommended that no federal assistance should be given to institutions that practised segregation. These recommendations were the most far-ranging and comprehensive proposals ever put forward by an American President and were to form the basis of civil rights issues for the next twenty years.

The President accepted the proposals which formed the basis of the civil rights programme he submitted to Congress in February 1948. He also kept faith by issuing an executive order which effectively ended segregation and discrimination in the armed services. Truman's association with the cause of civil rights created an uproar. The administration had affirmed again that there would be no deliberate reversal of the social reforms of the past fifteen years. It also acknowledged the electoral importance of the black vote and the willingness to risk the permanent defection of southerners from the ranks of the Democratic party. Truman had taken a calculated risk. In the unlikely event of obtaining civil rights legislation, he could claim the credit. If he failed, he could blame the recalcitrant Congress for failing to deliver legislation that advanced the cause of justice. Some critics accused him of moving too slowly and too reluctantly on this issue. He occasionally attended segregated meetings and diluted his proposals at election time. But Truman wanted to preserve the unity of the party if he could. If he could not, then he chose the path of civil rights reform. That path had its own political dividends. Whatever the case he could boast that he had moved to take the sting out of the tail of his international critics.

There was little legislative advance in the field of civil rights prior to 1954 when the Supreme Court handed down its momentous decision in *Brown v. Topeka Board of Education,* declaring segregation in the schools unconstitutional. Attempts to get serious legislative consideration of the resident's civil rights proposals were thwarted by the procedural powers of the House Rules Committee and the filibusters of opponents in the Senate. But advances were made; these were largely the result of administrative acts and judicial decisions. The military services moved towards integration under the watchful eye of the President's Committee on Equality of Treatment and Opportunity in the Armed Services. The momentum of integration in the forces increased with the outbreak of the Korean war. Segregation was found to be too complicated, too inefficient and, above all, too embarrassing. In the courts, momentum was building up to the complete destruction of legal segregation. In two important cases in 1950 concerning education, *Sweatt v. Painter* and *McLaurin v. Oklahoma State Regents,* the Supreme Court ruled that the separate facilities provided for black students in Texas and Oklahoma were unequal. Civil rights organizations now knew that segregation hung by a legal thread.

By and large the Truman administration wished to build up a record of social welfare legislation. The widening of the state's responsibilities could be seen as a reinforcement of its foreign policy. Liberal Democrats believed that the United States would be strengthened in its confrontation with the Soviet Union and in its leadership of Western Europe if it adopted a vitalized form of progressivism. In the ideological war with the Soviet Union the United States could not be tarred with the brush of social callousness. Capitalism had to be seen to be fair. In his 1949 State of the Union address Truman declared that 'Every segment of our population and every individual has a right to expect from our Government a fair deal'. The President wished to preserve the progressive impulse by calling for civil rights legislation, a 75 cent minimum wage, national medical insurance and extensive programmes of public housing and aid to education. They may not have liked his style and they shrunk at his occasional but necessary concessions, but liberals looked forward to a new age of reform, and Truman gave them reason to expect it. This refined version of New

Deal liberalism formed what Arthur Schlesinger Jnr. has called 'the vital centre'. It stood for a mixed economy, partial government planning, welfare programmes to provide a minimum level of economic security and the control of excessive concentrations of power. It was opposed to totalitarianism of any kind and endorsed the United States' policy of containing the Soviet Union.

The new responsibilities of power were acclaimed as a major change in the political consciousness of the nation and were seen as the apotheosis of the liberal dream. The safeguarding of democracy abroad reinforced democracy at home. Supporters of a strong national defence argued that high levels of military spending gave government a special and added interest in the promotion of full employment. The use of government contracts also created opportunities to enforce federal policies on employment practices and racial discrimination. But to some Americans the very consolidation and advancement of the New Deal posed a threat to their hope of a restoration of a market-led economy and a halt to the social engineering of postwar liberals.

The most forceful method employed by conservatives of checking the growth of federal government was the crusade against suspected communists within the United States. Some politicians and officials found that they could make considerable reputations for themselves by questioning the loyalty of prominent public figures. Senator Joseph McCarthy of Wisconsin was the most notorious witch-hunter – he found that his outrageous charges helped his political recognition to the extent that it gave rise to a new word in the vocabulary of American politics, McCarthyism. McCarthy may have been the most vicious inquisitor but he was not the only one. The concern about disloyalty and subversion affected all areas of public life. Yet it did not arouse that much public concern; problems of inflation and foreign policy worried people more. The McCarthyite phenomenon was the product of the convergence of various forces. The most immediate was the onset of the Cold War. Americans had expected to experience a sense of omnipotence arising from their powerful postwar position. Yet despite their atomic monopoly, which they enjoyed until 1949, the highest gross national product in the world and the relatively smooth transition from war to peace, they had been unable to stop the Soviet domination of Eastern Europe and to reverse the slide towards a communist victory in the Chinese Civil War. The most obvious explanation for these setbacks, namely that the United States could not control all events overseas or that the price of such control would be too high, was not always easily accepted. Incompetence was a tempting charge that was easily made and often indiscriminately levelled. Worse than that it was conceivable, in the eyes of some, that there had been a deliberate mishandling of the postwar challenges that bordered on the disloyal.

This view was fuelled by a number of largely unrelated revelations that were open to conspiratorial interpretations. Early in 1945, for example, extracts from classified State Department documents were discovered in a specialist journal on Far Eastern matters, *Amerasia*. Later in the year security officers broke into the offices of the journal and discovered a large number of classified documents in its possession. In 1948 Alger Hiss, a former State Department official and an assistant to Franklin Roosevelt at the Yalta conference, was accused before the House Committee on UnAmerican Activities by Whittaker Chambers, a confessed communist agent, of being a Soviett agent and of passing on secrets to the Soviets. In 1950 he was convicted of perjury in relation to the charge. The implication, of course, was that he was guilty. The Soviet Union's detonation of an atomic bomb in 1949, together with the arrest in February 1950 of British physicist Klaus Fuchs on charges of espionage, seemed to confirm the worst fears of those who were intent on finding proof of malfeasance in high places. Considerable political capital could be made from sensational charges of disloyalty in the upper echelons of government. It was a lesson that was not lost on men like Congressman Richard Nixon, who brought the Hiss case to light, and to Senator Joseph McCarthy of Wisconsin, who spearheaded the congressional investigations in the early 1950s. People would more easily remember their names if they were identified with scandalous revelations than if they were attached to a congressional committee or a trade bill.

It must not be assumed, however, that the Red Scare was simply the work of a few paranoid and disgruntled politicians. It was also the product of the reference in which the Cold War was conducted. It was not alien to the public discourse on foreign policy which extolled the virtues of a zealous defence of a liberal culture. For example, Clark M. Clifford, Special Counsel to President Truman, advised that opposition to the Soviet Union had to be combined with vigilance at home. 'Within the United States,' he wrote, 'communist penetration should be exposed and eliminated whenever the national security is endangered.' Common values and ideological mobilization were integral to the success of the new foreign policy. Containment required a sense of national purpose. Americans were taught by policy-makers that the survival of democracy at home was inextricably linked to the survival of democracy abroad. The doctrine of universalism meant that there could be no discrete parts in a liberal culture. Thus it was desirable to encourage policy-makers and opinion-makers to subscribe to the fundamental values of cold war America. A degree of conformity was necessary, as is the case in the prosecution of all wars.

It was not just the persistent badgering of right-wing Republicans that engendered the new uniformity. The administration itself nurtured the belief. In its quest for unanimity Truman dismissed Henry Wallace from the Cabinet in September 1946 for his outspoken criticism of the administration's policies towards the Soviet Union. In March 1947, in the same month that he enunciated the Truman Doctrine, the President implemented a permanent loyalty programme for civil servants. He did not believe that there were large numbers of disloyal employees. However, he did wish to steal the thunder of his critics who accused his administration of harbouring disloyal officials. Furthermore, he could not afford the embarrassment of revelations of risks to the national security. Truman's Executive Order of March 1947 required a loyalty investigation by a Loyalty Review Board of every employee entering government service. The standard for barring or dismissing an employee was that 'reasonable grounds exist for belief that the person involved is disloyal to the Government of the United States'. The criteria were loose and open to the wildest interpretations. It confused and treated without differentiation the very real problem of security in highly sensitive areas with the general problem of loyalty at all levels. Secretaries in cleaning departments simply do not need the same amount or the same kind of vetting as do physicists in nuclear laboratories. It provided few procedural safeguards and gave investigating officials unrestrained leeway in their judgements. Yet the loyalty programme raised an important issue. There is no reason why governments, universities or other public bodies should guarantee the right of employment irrespective of the personal views of its employees. Boys' schools are disinclined to hire homosexual teachers; pharmaceutical companies are likely to show little tolerance to salesmen who wax rhapsodic about homeopathic medicines. The guardians of the nation's security argued that irrespective of the wisdom of the United States' policy of containment, the policy could only be successfully implemented if it had the backing of its public servants. And they had a point.

Unfortunately for the postwar generation, the argument was put forward with little sense of judiciousness or restraint. The most notorious of the witch-hunters was Senator Joseph R. McCarthy who held the stage for four years with his demagogic and outrageous antics and accusations against government officials whose loyalty was not really doubtful. His fame began when he announced in a speech at Wheeling, West Virginia, that he possessed a list of names of 205 employees who were known by the Secretary of State to be communists and yet were still working there. These sensational charges were immediately publicized by the press and McCarthy knew he had hit upon an exciting issue. Within days he amended his charges. The numbers were whittled down almost daily and the charges switched from 'bad risks' to 'card-carrying' communists. Although his charges were wanton they could not be ignored. Mud sticks and McCarthy knew it. He used the Senate floor where he enjoyed congressional privilege to further his cause by enlarging his smear campaign. He elaborated on his charges but hardly convincingly. Three people 'with Soviet names' became 'three Soviets'. He told outright lies. Men with clean files were presented as subjects for investigation for known communist affiliation. He named names. They were thoroughly investigated by a Senate Committee and cleared. Yet for four years McCarthy and his supporters continued to level charges at individuals and to conduct inquisitions of public institutions, industries and labour unions. Honourable men were defamed. Anybody was fair game. Even General George Marshall, the former Secretary of State, did not escape vilification. McCarthy's henchmen became the custodians of the nation's intellectual and public life. They investigated labour unions, the film industry, the army and even the libraries of American embassies overseas. 'Subversive' literature was removed. There were stories that the works by Tom Paine and Thomas Jefferson were taken from embassy libraries. Nothing seemed sacred.

But the hysteria did not last. McCarthy exhausted his credibility and, with that exhaustion, the fervour for imposing conformity by ferreting out subversives waned. The demise of McCarthyism illustrates the point made earlier. The movement was ultimately ephemeral. It touched on a serious issue, the importance of closing ranks in organizations with a common purpose; but it tackled it with indiscriminate invective and almost wilful self-destructiveness. McCarthyism fell into disrepute. Its decline was probably hastened by the gradual distancing of the White House from its activities. Neither

President Truman nor President Eisenhower had ever supported the excesses of the inquisitors; indeed they detested McCarthy. But they provided a receptive framework for his insinuations in the rhetoric and justifications they employed in their conduct of foreign policy. Furthermore, they legitimated the distrust of dissidence of any kind in the loyalty programmes they set up and endorsed and in their tacit and sometimes explicit approval of the various measures taken to enforce political conformity. Their virtual silence over random dismissals from employment, the restrictions on the issue of passports to those under suspicions, and the registration of subversive organizations were read as tolerance. Eisenhower's selection of Richard Nixon as a running mate did not help the cause of libertarianism. But in the 1954 congressional elections the Republican party once again lost control of both houses of Congress. Conservative Republicans realized that there was no longer any premium in the continuing support of McCarthy. The elections were interpreted as a repudiation of McCarthy's tactics. His impugnings were simply not credible any more; television had brought the hysterical nature of his rantings into the homes of Americans. Republican leaders and the President moved against him. He was censured by the Senate in December 1954 and virtually silenced thereafter.

McCarthy seemed increasingly irrelevant. Americans had grown accustomed to the confrontation with the Soviet Union and, more important, now believed that that confrontation was better managed. The war in Korea had drawn to a satisfactory conclusion; in Iran the United States had supported the successful overthrow of the pro-Soviet Mossadeq regime and in Indochina military involvement had been avoided by Eisenhower's judiciousness. If there were any traitors in government they were not making their mark. Finally, the elections had shown that Americans were still broadly sympathetic to the expansion of welfare services that had been undertaken by Roosevelt and Truman. Eisenhower did not want to expand the authority of government but neither did he want to turn the clock back. Anti-communism at home had been a device for bringing the supporters of the New Deal and the associates of Roosevelt into disrepute. It may have destroyed the careers of individuals but it did not seriously dent the apparatus of state. If a modern conservative tradition was to be established, a basis other than anti-communism had to be found. Indeed a fitting epitaph to the McCarthyite era was to be found in the American response to the Soviet Union's launching of their first space satellite, *Sputnik*, in 1957. Americans reacted to it not by blaming the laxity or disloyalty of the nation's scientists and technicians, but by questioning its system of higher education.

The decade after Hiroshima was, for Americans, a decade of difficult adjustment. The United States was now the most powerful nation on earth. Its gross national product had grown from $213 billion in 1945 to nearly $400 billion a decade later, an increase of 86 percent; since 1941 the figure had trebled. It had achieved an economy of plenty despite prognoses of slump. It had committed $13 billion to the reconstruction of Europe and had seen that devastated continent emerge from the ashes. It possessed a nuclear arsenal, permanent fleets in the Mediterranean and the Pacific and had been instrumental in the formation of NATO. These developments had been undertaken with considerable soul-searching and had created the framework for the agony of McCarthyism. But what emerged was a polity that, despite reservations by the Eisenhower administration, accepted the necessity of providing some economic assistance to those who were unable to help themselves and continued the policy of containment. There was to be no turning back. There had been frustrations, disillusionment and some serious questioning. But the struggles over communist subversion, labour relations, the control of inflation and the civil rights of America's blacks illustrated that the nation's course was set. There were still sections of the community, primarily among the nation's poor, who felt that social progress was too selective and government responsibility insufficient. They did not share in the much vaunted new prosperity. The United States might have been, they argued, at the height of its power, but they did not feel the benefits of that power. They were determined to try and accelerate the change.

Further reading

William C. Berman, *The Politics of Civil Rights in the Truman Administration* (Columbus, OH, 1970).

David Caute, *The Great Fear: The Anti-Communist Purge Under Truman and Eisenhower* (London, 1978).

William Chafe, *The Unfinished Journey: America Since World War 2* (New York, 1986).

Robert J. Donovan, *Conflict and Crisis: The Presidency of Harry S. Truman, 1945-1948* (New York, 1977).

Robert J. Donovan, *Tumultuous Years: The Presidency of Harry S. Truman, 1949-1953* (New York, 1982)

Alonzo L. Hamby, *Beyond the New Deal: Harry S. Truman and American Liberalism* (New York, 1973).

5

The origins of the Cold War, 1945–1952

The end of the Second World War in August 1945 was greeted in the United States, as in other parts of the globe, with a combination of rejoicing, relief and sadness for those who fell. Americans were not foolish enough to believe that the Second World War had been a war to end all wars. That mistake would not be repeated. But they did not expect that within a few years of their victory over fascism, they would arm themselves against their former ally, the Soviet Union. Nor, if it comes to that, did they expect that Germany and Japan would be mainstays in their rivalry with the Soviets. Americans believed that they had learned some lessons from history. The principal one was that as a world power the United States would have to involve itself actively in world affairs. It would employ its full financial, intellectual and military might to realize the kind of world order that would serve and protect the national interest. Victory would be hollow unless the United States endeavoured to reconstruct the shattered world in such a way as to ensure a lasting peace and the prosperity of all nations, including itself. But it could only play a creative international role if it enjoyed the confidence of the other powers. Economic revival and international organizations would not in themselves promote peace. Such peace would remain elusive if international affairs were dominated by rivalry rather than co-operation. Thus the Truman administration set itself one overriding, primary goal. It strove to create the basis for a new world order that would simultaneously resurrect harmony and maintain the indisputable power that the United States had attained at end of the hostilities.

The Truman Administration developed three principal goals for the achievement of its policy aims. First it intended to prevent its former enemies, principally Germany and Japan, from ever attaining a position that would enable them to threaten international stability. This would entail the military occupation of their territory, followed by the development of new political systems that would prevent a resurgence of nationalistic militarism. The occupation of those countries by the army would also enable the United States to exert authority beyond their frontiers in neighbouring areas. The second element in the administration's strategy, though it was plain that it would not develop properly until 1947, was the provision of financial aid for the reconstruction of Europe. American policy makers recognized that economic hardship bred discontent. The war had resulted in the wholesale destruction of industry, the devastation of crops and livestock, the disruption of transportation and untold suffering among refugees, homeless families and the survivors of the holocaust. If means could be found of providing immediate relief and, later, aid for reconstruction, then a firm basis for the restoration of prosperity could be laid. Overseas aid would also, of course, benefit the American economy by boosting demand for home produced goods, although there is little evidence to suggest that this was a primary consideration. It was an incentive, not a motive. The third, and most immediate concern, was to iron out differences with its former allies, in particular the Soviet Union.

The ending of the war did not eliminate disagreements with the Soviet Union over the future of Eastern Europe, the issue of reparations from Germany or the scope of American influence in the Far East. If anything, it added a new urgency to these issues. For if diplomacy could not resolve them, then military power would, and in 1945, the United States did not envisage the use of direct military power or involvement to achieve its diplomatic goals. Overwhelmingly, Americans wanted to see a rapid demobilization of their armed forces. They wanted taxes cut, and, if there had to be sustained public expenditure, they wanted it spent on social welfare at home. Thus the President sought to continue Roosevelt's policies of seeking accommodation with the Soviets. Some historians have detected a shift in policy after Roosevelt's death. However, they have confused Truman's rhetorical style with the substance of his diplomacy. Truman did not have his predecessor's way with words, or, indeed, his patience. Yet he was willing in the early months of the postwar years to compromise in the hope of finding solutions.

The foreign policy of the Truman Administration was constrained by the normal forces of the American political system. Public opinion was undoubtedly more informed about international matters in 1945 than it had been in 1939. But there was a contradictory tension in public attitudes, a tension that was not easily resolved. Americans believed that their interests were best served by involving themselves in the new collective security organization, the United Nations, and by insisting that the postwar settlement should embody the principles of a free market and national self-determination. If these principles were rejected in the diplomatic exchanges that were to take place then the United States should tailor its military and economic supremacy to realize these goals. There was little support for surrendering any advantage in the hope of gaining the confidence of the Soviet Union. For example, a poll in August 1945 showed that over 70 per cent of the public wanted to retain exclusive possession of the atomic bomb, and not turn it over to an international body. At the same time, however, Americans called for rapid demobilization, so that their men could return home as soon as possible. Congressmen were besieged with letters calling for the quick return of sons and husbands from the war front. The public wanted the government to assume a tougher stance with the Soviets but was not prepared to provide the means for backing it up. Thus Truman faced a difficult challenge. He had to mobilize consent for a foreign policy which Americans endorsed but did not want to pay for.

Despite some tough talking, Truman had not made up his mind about the Soviets by the time the war drew to a close. His advisers believed that the monopoly on atomic power could be traded for concessions from the Soviets in Eastern Europe and elsewhere. They understood that the Soviets were desperately short of raw materials and capital for reconstruction purposes and hoped that they might still turn to the West for aid. Above all, it was felt that Stalin was a realist and would be amenable to negotiation. James F. Byrnes, Secretary of State from June 1945 to January 1947, went to Moscow in December 1945 to meet with Stalin in the hope of clearing up some outstanding issues. Byrnes had been a close associate of Roosevelt and still carried his mantle: personal meetings and the occasional grand gesture would, in his view, bend the Soviets. At the Moscow meeting he wanted to resolve the impasse that had arisen over Soviets policy in the Balkans. Stalin made some symbolic concessions. In return Byrnes outlined his plan for a United Nations Atomic Energy Commission, which would provide for exchanges of scientific information and limit the use of atomic weapons. When Byrnes returned to Washington a storm broke out. Congressional leaders accused Byrnes of trading the United States' most effective military and diplomatic weapon for worthless promises. The President was less concerned about the details of the agreements but realized that Byrnes had antagonized important opinion leaders. Truman could not afford such estrangement. The political message seemed clear. The time for concessions was over and the United States had to develop its own resources and rely less on diplomacy to realize the world order it so desired. Truman learned that there were no political dividends to be earned in dealing with the Soviets. Indeed, one of the notable characteristics of the early Cold War was the rapid decline in diplomacy as a vehicle of serving the national interest. By the beginning of 1946 policy makers presumed that American power was best served through unilateral action and the formation of close ties with its allies and potential allies.

The United States came to realise that in certain parts of the globe it was virtually powerless. In Poland and Rumania elections were postponed and, when they were finally held, were exercises in the ratification of hand-picked candidates. The United States recognized the limits of its own power and was unwilling to force the Soviets' hand in Eastern Europe. It simply did not consider it worth the risk. In China, which was racked by civil war between Chiang-Kai-shek's Nationalists and the communists, the administration used whatever diplomatic suasion was available to bring the warring sides together. However, it was unwilling to make any substantial commitment. Despite pressure from the Republican right and some wishful thinking among some of Truman's advisers, the administration decided to limit its assistance to missions of conciliation and limited economic aid. Again, it knew it did not have the resources to affect the outcome of the conflict and it had few illusions about the reliability of Chiang. It knew, and the final victory of the communist forces in January 1949 confirmed this view, that American power would have to be exerted in the Far East through other client nations. A reconstructed Japan and a strong American influence in places like Korea and Indochina could serve the same purpose.

The federal government had no doubt that it should consolidate its influence wherever possible and that it should use all reasonable means to secure regimes that broadly shared the political and economic values of the United States. It also did not want and could not sustain full military mobilization to realize these ambitions. Public opinion would not support it. People wanted their men home and their taxes cut. Anyway, they were not conditioned to peacetime militarization. The administration faced two problems: how to achieve these goals and how to identify the precise nature of the Soviet threat. After all, if Eastern Europe or Korea had been of little importance to national security only a decade earlier, how could the United States justify its sudden interest?

The most comprehensive and methodical statement came from the pen of George Kennan, U.S. Chargé d'Affaires in Moscow and the architect of the policy that soon came to be known as containment. In an 8,000 word telegram sent from Moscow to the State Department on 22 February 1946 Kennan argued that the Soviets were ignorant of the outside world. They believed that they were surrounded by hostile capitalists with whom they would one day have to fight. It was thus in their interest to weaken and destabilize the West to prepare for that fight. The United States would have to respond by creating a national ideology that was an equivalent counter to communism. There should be no separation between domestic and foreign policy. 'We must formulate,' Kennan said, 'and put forward for other nations a much more positive and constructive picture of [sic] sort of world we would like to see than we have put forward in the past. It is not enough to urge people to develop political processes similar to our own ... They are seeking guidance rather than responsibilities. We should be better able than Soviets to give them this. And unless we do, Soviets certainly will.' In short he was calling for firm and clear overseas commitments based on a sound ideological footing. The give and take of wartime diplomacy no longer made sense. Americans had to learn to believe in themselves and to transmit that faith to others.

The United States then began to plan for major involvement overseas. It required careful preparation. As has been emphasized, Americans were looking to cuts in military expenditure and did not at that time envisage that the presence of troops in Europe would be permanent. The first major turning point came in February 1947 when Britain informed the United States that it planned to terminate all aid to Greece and Turkey at the end of March. Greece was in the throes of a bloody civil war between its conservative government and communist-led guerillas. The State Department accepted Britain's belief that Greece in particular was of vital strategic importance to the western world and believed that the guerillas were agents of the Soviet Union. The State Department, invigorated by the appointment of General George Marshall as Secretary of State, was convinced that the United States should fill the vacuum left by Britain. Failure to do so would result in a domino effect, and could leave large parts of the Near

East in communist hands. This would have a debilitating impact on Western Europe, which found it difficult enough to maintain democratic government in the face of material shortages, labour unrest and shortfalls in financial liquidity. The President was in no doubt that the United States should provide economic aid to alleviate the situation. 'It means U.S. going into European politics. It means the greatest selling job ever,' he observed. Truman knew that aid to Greece and Turkey was just a prologue to a larger commitment to the reconstruction of Western Europe as a whole. If he could get Congress to grant aid to the Greeks, he could get it to assume responsibility for nations that were more important to America's security. Thus on 12 March 1947 he enunciated his celebrated Truman Doctrine, which called for $400 million in aid. He used shock therapy. 'At the present moment in world history,' he declared, 'nearly every nation must choose between alternative ways of life. The choice is often not a free one ... I believe it must be the policy of the United States to support free people who are resisting attempted subjugation by armed minorities or by outside pressures.' It was the official declaration of cold war.

The Truman Doctrine served a variety of purposes. First, it enshrined the principle that even in peacetime foreign policy would be high on the political agenda. It would be presented to the electorate in simple, comprehensible terms so that major decisions would carry the added weight of full public support. Second, it performed the crucial function, already referred to, of providing Americans with a special sense of nationality. Foreign policy was now not just the defence of trade and territory but also a defining component of national character. It confirmed Americans in their liberal heritage. Third, it signalled to the Soviet Union that the United States had also developed an ideological rationale for its interventions overseas. That rationale would form the basis of future policy calculations in both Washington and Moscow. It was hoped that the Soviets now knew where they stood with the Americans.

The Truman Doctrine also eased the way for the economic containment of the Soviet Union, the corner-stone of American policy in 1947. The administration had largely accepted the premises of Kennan's analysis of Soviet behaviour. Policy makers believed that the Kremlin combined realism and opportunism with a fundamental adherence to Marxist–Leninist ideology. That meant that if an opportunity arose for the Soviets in Western Europe they would not hesitate to seize it. It was vital, therefore, to build up democratic institutions in Western

Europe and to shore up the national economies in order to insure peace and prosperity. Americans were also alarmed at the lack of direction in the world economy. They realized that revived capitalist economies would not emerge from the ashes of war that easily. The nations of Western Europe found it almost impossible to break out of the doldrums of dollar shortages and lack of capital for investment in the internal economic infrastructure. They resorted to restrictive trade regulations and bilateral arrangements with individual trading partners. Furthermore, vital resources remained unexploited because of political prejudice. The British and American zones of Germany, now combined for administrative purposes into one zone, Bizonia, still scarcely functioned above subsistence level. Any major aid to the Germans would be seen as hostile by the Soviets and to some extent by the French. But the Germans possessed unused resources, particularly coal, which could be employed to revive the economies of Europe. A means had to be found, therefore, of encouraging a German revival and harnessing that revival with a programme that would help Europe maintain its capitalist character. The United States could kill two birds with one stone. It could help get Europe back on its feet and hopefully outbid the powerful socialist and communist movements which thrived on the uncertainty of the times. It would also, in the process, be in a position to influence and shape the direction of the emerging economies.

It was within this context that Secretary of State George Marshall made his celebrated speech at Harvard University in June when he called upon all European governments to initiate a programme for a co-ordinated reconstruction. He pledged the United States' generous support and aid for the programme. A Policy Planning Staff paper of July 1947 spelled out American interests quite clearly: 'The United States people have a very real economic interest in Europe. This stems from Europe's role in the past as a market and as a major source of supply for a variety of products and services. But beyond this, the traditional concept of U.S. security has been predicated on the sort of Europe now in jeopardy.' Marshall's offer of aid was extended to all the European nations but the Soviets and their clients in Eastern Europe understood that the European Recovery Programme, or Marshall Plan as it came to be known, was designed to create an integrated world economy. If the Soviets joined the scheme, they would effectively destroy their own economic system. So the Marshall Plan became a Western European programme. American power was now conjoined with the fate of Europe. It had become indivisible.

The Marshall Plan marked the highpoint of economic containment. The administration hoped that once the Soviet Union perceived the determination of the United States to bolster the economies of those nations that were crucial to its interests, it would temper its political and territorial ambitions. It must be emphasized again that after the war the United States hoped to reduce its military commitments. Economic aid was seen as a substitute for military defence. If Western Europe could be strengthened it would ward off the politics of discontentment and create sufficient wealth to pay for its own defence. But while the Marshall Plan – some $13 billion in aid was provided over a four year period – undoubtedly succeeded in reviving the economic health of Europe it failed, in the United States' eyes, to curb the advance of communism. As a result of that failure the United States resorted to containment by military means. A number of separate events and crises occurred which caused the Truman administration to reevaluate its military posture. The first was one that was of its own making. The attempt to consolidate its power in Western Europe, including in Germany, was bound to evoke a parallel response from the Kremlin. Stalin regarded the European Recovery Programme as a brazen attempt to isolate the Soviets. In September 1947 he responded in kind by organizing the Communist Information Bureau (Cominform), which aimed to facilitate trade between the communist nations of Eastern Europe. This was the first step in a fresh campaign to consolidate the Eastern bloc. Then in February 1948 a crisis emerged in Czechoslovakia. Twelve of the twenty-six members of the Czech cabinet resigned in the hope of obtaining a dissolution of the government. They miscalculated. Instead, the communists under Clement Gottwald seized power and Czechoslovakia's experiment with straddling East and West came to a sudden end. Four months later in June the world's attention was focused on the city of Berlin. The Soviet Union decided to cut the western sectors off from the western zone of Germany. They had recognized that the inclusion of Marshall Aid to Germany ended all intentions to pay reparations to the Soviet Union and to conduct a joint occupation policy. The West planned to build a new German state; the introduction of a currency reform was an irreversible step in that direction. When it announced that the new currency would also be circulated in Berlin's western sectors the Soviet Union imposed a dramatic blockade of rail, road and water routes to Berlin. This left the inhabitants of the western sectors at the mercy of the Soviets for fuel and food.

The blockade posed the first major challenge to the President. If he left the Berliners to succumb, the United States' credibility as the guarantor of Western Europe's security would look hollow. If he challenged the Soviets directly, he faced the possibility of a military engagement. He chose to act prudently but firmly. He supported the airlift of vital supplies and hinted that if the Soviets attempted to shoot down relief aircraft, the response would be escalated. The Soviets let the airlift proceed. The city survived and a year later the Soviet Union called off the blockade. The United States drew its own lesson from the Berlin crisis. While its offer of economic aid had given encouragement to European reconstruction, it had not been an effective deterrent against the Soviet Union. The administration concluded that militarization would have to be adopted as an essential tool in its containment policy.

It was not only in Europe that tough talk and economic aid proved inadequate to the task. In the Chinese Civil War Mao Zedong's communist forces made gain after gain as territory previously held by the Nationalist government fell to Mao's forces. The United States had tried to stem the tide but not with any real expectations of success. Various missions had been sent to China to try and reconcile the two sides. But these failed to get Chiang to implement reforms and did nothing to take the sting out of the tail of the communists. After pressure from the Republicans, and for the sake of consistency, a China Aid Act was passed in 1948, which provided for $400 million in economic and military aid to the beleaguered Nationalists. But it was too late and everybody knew it. After Chiang fled in permanent exile to Formosa in January 1949, the administration published a 'White Paper' on China and admitted that the outcome of the Chinese Civil War had been 'beyond the control' of the United States. The administration believed that thenceforth it would have to concentrate its resources in those areas of Asia that were still within American control or susceptible to its influence. Communism seemed on the march everywhere and dollars alone had been insufficient to halt it. And when, to crown it all, the Soviet Union successfully detonated its own atomic bomb in August 1949 the United States realized that only military deterrence would preserve American power.

The United States began the process which turned it into the most formidable military power on earth. It sought to possess sufficient mastery over the ever-changing conditions throughout the world. The

Soviet Union was presented as a threat to the balance of power and to national security. The Europeans had learned that economic aid did not automatically bring military security in its wake. Indeed the reintegration of Germany had shown that it created military insecurity. The Czech and Berlin crises had convinced governments on both sides of the Atlantic that the United States should join Europe in its efforts at mutual defence and should help it rearm. The new Secretary of State in 1949, Dean Acheson, collaborated closely with the Senate to create what became the United States' first major permanent alliance. Under the terms of the North Atlantic Treaty Organization (NATO), which was ratified by the Senate in July 1949, each signatory pledged 'individually and in concert with the other parties, such action as it deems necessary, including the use of armed force, to restore and maintain the Security of the North Atlantic area'. The administration insisted that the treaty did not automatically commit the United States to war in Europe. But this was not very convincing, particularly when American troops were stationed in Europe as part of NATO's forces. NATO was one of the most far-reaching commitments the United States had ever made. The United States now permanently underwrote Europe's security and set in train the military integration, including Germany, of the western nations.

The formation of NATO was just the beginning of the American arms build-up. In January 1950 the President asked Secretary of State Dean Acheson to undertake a major review of the nation's military policy. Acheson turned the task over to Paul Nitze, the new director of the State Department's Policy Planning Staff. Nitze's study group attempted to cover every major aspect of national security policy. His endeavour resulted in what was probably the most important peacetime strategic reassessment that had ever been made. The completed study, a seventy page, single-spaced document, was submitted to Truman on 7 April 1950, and given the forgettably coded title, *NSC-68*. *NSC-68* was a systematic attempt to integrate political, economic, and military policies into a comprehensive national security plan. *NSC-68* claimed that the United States' 'military strength is becoming dangerously inadequate'. It presented a world picture in which the United States and 'free institutions' elsewhere were being 'mortally challenged' by the Soviet Union. It pointed to the high proportion of national income spent by the Soviets on military requirements and to the Soviet Union's atomic weapons. It warned that American allies would not be able to defend themselves in the event of war. It called for a major rearmament programme and argued that the nation could almost treble defence expenditure without impairing current living standards. It pointed out that the United States relied overwhelmingly on deterrence. This was not appropriate in local disputes where the Soviet Union would risk intervention since the United States was ill-prepared for small, conventional skirmishes and would scarcely risk all-out war for an objective that was not central to the national security. It called for a rapid increase in conventional forces as well as the production and stockpiling of thermonuclear weapons. Above all, *NSC-68* insisted that an expansion of military expenditure would stimulate the economy. It argued that an arms programme would serve the national interest in all respects. Americans and their allies had to learn that 'the cold war is in fact a real war in which the survival of the free world is at stake'. The arms race had now become an adjunct of economic policy and the political galvanization of the nation. Peace and prosperity would be sought by preparing for war.

Truman approved the proposals but hesitated about their cost. However, his reservations were thrown to the wind by a dramatic development which made the international diagnosis of *NSC-68* seem prophetic and its recommendations urgent. On 24 June 24 1950 Truman was shocked to learn that North Korea had invaded South Korea. The offensive came as a total surprise. There had been reports of troop movements along the 38th parallel which divided the two nations but they had not been taken seriously in Washington. The attack presented a serious challenge to the United States. Korea had been divided after the war, with the Soviets occupying the North and the Americans the South. The American occupation was marked by support of conservative groups under the leadership of Syngman Rhee. In 1948 elections were held in the South and a new government under Rhee was formed. But that government was unstable, despite aid from the United States. There were strikes, mutinies and demonstrations in protest against the nepotism and political censorship of the regime. The United States was committed to its support, at least in principle. After all, the republic of South Korea had been formed under American tutelage and acted as a bulwark against the North which enjoyed military superiority. However, the administration had embarked upon a major review of its commitments overseas. It had agreed that priority should be given to those areas which were essential to the avoidance of a strategic defeat in the event of a full-scale war. Its principal zones of interest were in Western Europe and Japan. As a consequence, American troops were withdrawn from South Korea in mid-1949. The continuing occupation of Japan was considered sufficient for maintaining its influence in the Far East. Even General Douglas MacArthur had agreed. American strategists thought in terms of a general war, not a limited one. And anyway nobody thought that South Korea was worth taking. In a widely publicized statement in January 1950 Secretary Acheson had defined the United States' 'defensive perimeter' in the Far East; that imaginary line excluded both Formosa and South Korea. The American attempt to sharpen its areas of defined interest may have encouraged the Soviet Union to turn a blind eye to the military mobilization occurring in North Korea. It probably had little effect on the North Koreans themselves who wanted political unification and an end to border hostilities.

President Truman did not seriously consider any alternatives other than a military intervention to resist the North Koreans. This seemed particularly urgent as North Korean troops swept south, occupying the capital, Seoul, and pushing back South Korean troops towards a corner in the southern tip of the peninsula. The destiny of Korea was no longer considered to be part of the China problem or a residue of territorial disputes following the Second World War. What was now at stake was the very credibility of containment policy and the commitments associated with it. Policy makers had to make a crucial decision: should the United States become a permanent force in the Far East? They had originally calculated that the occupation of Japan and the maintenance of Chiang in China would be sufficient to uphold American power in Asia. But the victory of the communists in China had meant that the United States relied more heavily for its military security on its general posture towards communism, the growth of capitalist economies in the region and the authority that emanated from its presence in Japan. That assumption faced its most serious challenge from the North Koreans. Thus Truman's decision to order General MacArthur to come to the help of the fast collapsing Rhee government was more than just an attempt to demonstrate the nation's commitment to its client regimes. It signified that the Truman Doctrine was now a global doctrine and that the full force of American power would be used to maintain the strategic balance in the Far East. The series of decisions that accompanied Truman's order to MacArthur to use all the ground, air and naval forces at his command demonstrated the United States' determination to maintain a *Pax Americana* in the Pacific and Far East. The Seventh fleet was ordered into the Formosa

Strait to prevent the Chinese Nationalists and Communists from extending the war. If Formosa had once felt uncertain about the extent of the American commitment, it need do so no more. Extra military aid was also immediately extended to the Philippines and to Indo-china. Truman was quite clear in his own mind that the stakes were not confined to the Korean peninsula but to the whole of Asia.

The American involvement in the war in Korea confirmed the extension of power that had taken place. The United States now posed as the protector of the non-communist world. The President had hoped that the Korean intervention would be a limited operation. When the war escalated, he could justifiably claim that the Americans were serving the United Nations, which had endorsed the action. (This fortunate endorsement had been made possible only by the absence of the Soviet delegation in the Security Council, which it had boycotted over the UN's decision to allow the Chinese Nationalists to continue to occupy the permanent seat.) But warfare can only remain limited if both sides want it that way and if the military operations are deliberately restrained. The war did not remain limited for long. General MacArthur managed to break the North Korean advance by combining a brilliant amphibious landing at Inchon in the enemy's rear with a break-out of his beleaguered troops around the port of Pusan. By 1 October 1950, the UN forces had destroyed half the communist forces and had reached the 38th parallel. It was at this point that objectives became confused and the war escalated into a major land war. MacArthur, with the President's approval, pushed north in the hope of destroying North Korean forces and achieving unification. In November he advanced towards the Yalu River on China's border and there fell into a trap. The Chinese crossed the river, cut off some of his forces and forced the remainder to retreat with considerable losses. Chinese troops retook the North Korean capital, Pyongyang, crossed the 38th parallel, and quickly captured Seoul. It was like a repeat scenario. The war had now become a great power conflict and for the next two and a half years the two sides dug in while they tried to extricate themselves with sufficient honour.

The changing military fortunes in Korea forced the Truman Administration to revise its war aims. After the Chinese counter-attack and the retreat south, the administration realised that a cease-fire and a return to the status quo ante bellum, a divided Korea, was now the most realistic ambition. MacArthur disagreed. He believed that the United Nations' reverses, which he sometimes exaggerated, were due

to Washington's insistence on restraining his miliary tactics and
controlling the composition of the troops. He wanted authority for an
air and naval bombardment of China and the full use of Nationalist
forces from Formosa in both Korea and in diversionary action against
the Chinese mainland. He believed he could defeat China. 'There is
no substitute for victory,' he proclaimed in a letter that was read out
loud in the House of Representatives. He invited a bitter conflict with
the administration by openly publicizing his differences. The President
relieved him of his command for insubordination. The war settled
down to a long slog under the command of General Matthew
Ridgway. Attempts were made to break the stalemate around the
peace table, but a peace was to be as elusive as a decisive military
engagement. The armies got stuck in the mountainous terrain of
central Korea. It was only in 1953, some three years and 142,000
casualties later, that the deadlock was broken by Truman's successor,
Dwight Eisenhower.

The Korean war left two lasting lessons. First, it convinced the
United States that it had to possess a credible defence establishment.
It served to validate the warnings of *NSC-68* and so eased the way for
the implementation of its proposals for rearmament. A peace treaty
was prepared for Japan, the number of men in arms rose from about
1.5 million in 1950 to 3.5 million in 1953, research proceeded on the
development of the hydrogen bomb, the method of raising defence
contracts was eased and the overseas military aid programme was
extended. In 1953 the United States devoted 13.8 per cent of its gross
national product to defence, compared to 4.6 per cent in 1950. The
United States had become a fully fledged military power. Its national
security could only be guarded, policy makers argued, if the United
States was geared for war. The Soviets could fight by proxy. The
United States had to prepare itself in those areas of the world where
Soviet influence was still slight or invisible, and not just in the
strongpoints where the nation's major security interests lay. Arms and
firm military commitments would, hopefully, obviate the likelihood of
war against the communists. But their employment would no longer
be a matter of extended debate.

The second lesson, and it was one that was learned by Eisenhower
but not by his successors in the 1960s, was that the United States'
ability to determine the outcome of civil conflict in the Third World
was limited. Or, to be more accurate, it was limited by the military
means which were deemed practicable. The United States might have

been able to effect the unification of Korea, but only at unacceptable risk, the possibility of war with the Soviet Union. Military flexibility still had to be primarily deterrent in character. It was for this reason that Eisenhower came to value secret intelligence operations over direct intervention, particularly in cases where the outcome of such intervention was in doubt. Eisenhower recognized that while American power was formidable, it was not omnipotent. Such a realisation kept him away from direct intervention in Indochina. Eisenhower did not want another Korean stalemate. The United States was at the pinnacle of its power. In 1953 its gross national product was $365 billion; it possessed numerical superiority over the Soviet Union in nuclear weapons. But like all power, it had its limits. Arms and money could reinforce its allies, but they could not change the world. The United States would spend the next two decades in an education, sometimes painful, on the precise extent of those limits.

Further reading

John L. Gaddis, *The United States and the Origins of the Cold War, 1941-1947* (New York and London, 1972).

Joyce and Gabriel Kolko, *The Limits of Power: The World and United States Foreign Policy, 1945-1954* (New York, 1972).

Charles Mee, *The Marshall Plan* (New York, 1984).

William Stueck, *The Road to Confrontation: American Policy Towards China and Korea, 1947-1950* (Chapel Hill, NC, 1987).

Hugh Thomas, *Armed Truce: The Beginnings of the Cold War, 1945-1946* (London, 1986).

Daniel Yergin, *Shattered Peace: The Origins of the Cold War and the National Security State* (Boston, 1977).

6

Years of affluence, 1952-1960

The United States during the early 1950s was riven by political turmoil. The Korean War had reached the point of stalemate, labour disputes seemed to be undermining the economy, charges of subversion were commonplace and corruption appeared to be widespread. Caught in a maelstrom which he had little chance of calming, the political standing of President Truman was rapidly eroded. After twenty years of Democratic control of the White House, the country was ready for new leadership. As a Republican slogan in the 1952 election proclaimed, it was 'time for a change'. Change when it came, however, was to prove more stylistic than substantive. The New Deal, the Fair Deal and the emergence of the United States as a superpower in the aftermath of the Second World War had generated certain expectations about the role of the federal government which were not easily changed. Foremost among such expectations was the belief that the federal government should bear some responsibility for the welfare of its citizens.

The principle that the federal government should assume responsibility for the welfare of the citizens of the United States was accepted by both General Eisenhower and his Democratic opponent in the 1952 election, Governor Adlai E. Stevenson of Illinois. In fact, Eisenhower's nomination at the Republican Convention in Chicago, where he defeated Senator Robert Taft of Ohio, a leading conservative critic of both the New Deal and the Fair Deal, signalled the Republican Party's acceptance of the public philosophy espoused by Roosevelt, and an acknowledgement of the United States' new role in the world. During the campaign, however, Eisenhower made no promises regarding the introduction of new social programmes. Rather, he limited himself to a pledge to clean up 'the mess in Washington' and a promise to go to Korea to secure 'an early and honorable' peace. Governor Stevenson spoke eloquently about the threat posed to the

United States by poverty at home and war abroad, and tried to convince the voters that although the struggle against these problems was costly it was necessary. But it was all to no avail. The majority of Americans wanted to forget about the problems of the underprivileged. Stevenson could not hope to match the popularity of a war hero who had been in the public eye for over a decade, and was defeated in the election. Eisenhower received 33,936,000 popular and 442 electoral college votes to Stevenson's 27,314,000 popular and 89 electoral college votes.

Victory on this scale was a personal triumph for Eisenhower, and one which he was to repeat four years later. Support for Eisenhower, however, did not prove to be transferable to Republican candidates in general. Although Eisenhower's victory in 1952 was accompanied by the capture of both chambers of Congress by the Republicans, albeit by the barest of margins, such gains did not last. The Democrats regained control of Congress in the mid-term elections of 1954, and went on to consolidate their hold over the legislature in the elections of 1956 and 1958. Such results meant that Eisenhower was never able to enjoy the luxury of large, sympathetic majorities in Congress. Throughout his term as President he was forced to seek bipartisan support for his legislative programme.

The fate of Eisenhower's legislative programme provides a perfect illustration of the extent to which the expectations and structures of the New Deal, together with the geopolitical realities of the country's superpower status, created the basic framework within which all political discourse in the United States has had to take place. Calling his programme 'dynamic conservatism' Eisenhower placed considerable emphasis upon reducing the national budget. Again and again he warned of the dangers of 'creeping socialism', 'huge bureaucracies' and budget deficits, and sought to cut spending on both domestic programmes and national security. His success in achieving such objectives, however, was limited by the structural rigidities of the political system created by Roosevelt. Although Eisenhower managed to abolish the Reconstruction Finance Corporation, end wage and price controls and reduce farm subsidies, long-term radical change proved to be impossible. Attempts to reduce government spending were unsuccessful as more and more groups turned to the federal government for redress of their grievances. Throughout the 1950s both government spending and the size of the budget deficit rose.

In many respects the legislation of the Eisenhower years may be viewed as an extension of the New Deal and Fair Deal. To the great relief of American liberals, Eisenhower accepted the welfare state and agreed to modest expansion in some social programmes. Amendments to the Social Security Act in 1954 and 1956 provided coverage to occupational groups which had previously been excluded; they included farmers, state and local government employees, physicians and those serving in the armed services. Further amendments in 1958 provided a substantial increase in benefits to those receiving old-age, veteran's and disability assistance. The Minimum Wage Act (1955) increased the minimum hourly wage from 75 cents to one dollar. The National Defense Education Act (1958) authorized the expenditure of $887 million over a four year period for the improvement of American education. Later congressional action extended the measure for another two years at an additional cost of $500 million. The federal government's commitment to public works was also confirmed with the enactment of the St. Lawrence Seaway Act (1954) which authorized the building of a system of locks and canals to connect the Great Lakes to the Atlantic, and the Interstate Highways Act (1956) which appropriated $33.5 billion to build a national network of roads.

The Interstate Highways Act (1956) was one of the most important acts passed during the Eisenhower years. Not only did it facilitate a dramatic improvement in the mobility of the American people, but it also provided an enormous boost to the car industry. As the 1950s came to an end, the car had clearly established itself as king of the American landscape. Freeways, multistorey carparks, shopping centres and drive-in restaurants, cinemas and banks all catered to the motorist. Cars also became an important status symbol. They grew longer and sprouted tailfins which served no purpose other than to enhance the self-esteem of the driver. To meet the almost insatiable demand for new cars, the automobile industry based in Detroit expanded dramatically. By 1960 approximately one in seven American workers was employed in a job either directly or indirectly connected to the automobile industry.

The increased mobility which resulted from an improved road system and greater car production allowed many Americans to leave the cities for the suburbs. Suburbia met a need for cheap, affordable housing. A baby boom in the aftermath of the Second World War caused the American population to soar. Between 1940 and 1955 the population of the United States grew from 130 million to 165 million people. The need to accommodate this population growth was met by the almost overnight appearance of suburbs. In the East, housing tracts with names like 'Crystal Stream' and 'Stonybrook' sprang up. In the West, a Spanish motif was more in order, and the new suburbs were given names like 'Villa Serena' and 'Tierra Vista'. Whatever their names, however, the new communities proved irresistible. By the end of the 1950s, one quarter of the American population had moved to the suburbs.

Although the growth of the suburbs met an immediate demand for housing, movement on such a large scale was to generate significant problems in the future. Most of those who moved to the suburbs were affluent whites. Left behind were the poor and black who were to find it increasingly difficult to obtain work as industry also began to move to the suburbs. The result was widespread poverty and deprivation in the cities which would explode in the race riots of the 1960s. In short, the growth of suburbia would tear the social fabric of the United States apart.

Whatever his own personal views on the role of the federal government, the fact that Eisenhower accepted the enactment of amendments which increased the cover provided by the Social Security Act, and actively promoted the building of the St. Lawrence Seaway and the national network of interstate highways, served to legitimize the New Deal. For the first time, a Republican President was agreeing to measures which conformed with the federal government's new ascendancy in public life. Nowhere was this conformation more apparent than in the area of civil rights. In his championing of civil rights Eisenhower pushed the New Deal to its logical conclusion. Just as the National Labor Relations Act (1935) provided federal help to the labour movement, so Eisenhower sought to improve the position of another disadvantaged group, namely the country's black population.

The fact that the civil rights movement looked towards the federal government in general, and the President in particular, for redress of their grievances is testimony to the extent to which Franklin D. Roosevelt and Harry Truman had managed to transform public expectations of the role of government. By stressing the 'nationalism' of American life, Roosevelt ensured that problems which had hitherto been regarded as falling within the domain of the state governments were propelled into the White House for resolution. Truman's championing of civil rights had also served to focus attention on the White House. The fate of the civil rights movement during the 1950s, however, also reveals the extent to which public expectations of what the President could achieve were far greater than what was actually possible. Although the President was the focus of public expectations he had to act within a political system in which his power was limited. Not only did he have to share power at the federal level with Congress and the Supreme Court, but it was by no means certain that any decision taken at the national level would in fact be implemented by the states. Such realities were to dominate Eisenhower's approach to the problem of civil rights.

In those areas where he was able to act unchecked by the other branches of government, Eisenhower moved quickly to support the civil rights movement. During the first three years of his presidency he issued executive orders which desegregated public services in Washington DC, naval yards and veterans' hospitals. On the other hand, where he was less certain of success Eisenhower tended to move circumspectly. He was unwilling, for example, to waste precious political capital by repeating the unsuccessful efforts of the Truman Administration to force civil rights legislation through a Congress dominated by southern Democrats. Thus, although his administration would eventually see the enactment of the first Civil Rights Act since 1875, he preferred to avoid a confrontation with Congress, and instead supported the battle for civil rights which was taking place in the courts. Throughout the 1950s the Justice Department provided valuable support to those bringing anti-discrimination suits before the courts, and in some of the more momentous cases Administration officials engaged in behind-the-scenes lobbying of the Supreme Court in an effort to obtain a favourable judgement.

By far the most important civil rights case heard by the Supreme Court during the 1950s was *Brown v. Board of Education of Topeka, Kansas* (1954). In this case the Court ruled that separate educational facilities for blacks were inherently unequal. This ruling reversed an earlier ruling in the case *Plessy v. Ferguson* (1896) that separate facilities for blacks were constitutional so long as they were of an equal standard to those provided for white children. In rejecting the 'separate but equal' doctrine the new Chief Justice, Earl Warren, declared that 'in the field of public education the doctrine of "separate but equal" has no place. Separate educational facilities are inherently unequal, depriving the plaintiffs of the equal protection of the laws.' Warren argued that segregated facilities generate in black children 'a feeling of inferiority ... that may affect their hearts and minds in a way unlikely ever to be undone'. One year later the Court ordered that the desegregation of public schools should begin 'with all deliberate speed'. In issuing such an order the Court was setting an important precedent: it was initiating public policy without the backing of an Act of Congress. While future critics would question the Court's right to embark upon this course of action, in the short term the problem for the Court was how to enforce its decision.

White reaction to *Brown* was initially calm. However, as token integration began in states such as Virginia that had separate systems, so the opposition to desegregation grew. Citizens Councils were created to preserve segregation throughout the South, and in 1955 Senator Harry F. Byrd of Virginia made a call for 'Massive Resistance' to attempt to overturn segregation laws. Further opposition to desegregation came in 1956 when Senator Sam Ervin of North Carolina obtained the support of 101 southern members of Congress for a 'Southern Manifesto' which denounced *Brown* as 'a clear abuse of judicial power' and vowed to fight court-ordered desegregation by all legal means. Among the legal means used by the southern states to resist desegregation were 'interposition' statutes which declared *Brown* to be of no effect, and statutes which were superficially neutral but which resulted in the separation of school children by race. So successful were such devices that by the end of 1956 not a single school had been desegregated in six southern states and only token segregation had occurred in the others.

The problem of enforcement came to the fore at Little Rock, Arkansas. In September 1957 the Board of Education of Little Rock agreed to let nine black students enrol at one of the city's high schools. On the pretext, however, that there would be widespread violence if the students were admitted to classes, Governor Orval Faubus of Arkansas called out the National Guard to prevent the students from enrolling. A few days later a court order forced Governor Faubus to withdraw the National Guard, but a taunting, riot-prone mob prevented the black students from gaining access to the school. President Eisenhower responded to this breakdown in public order by sending a thousand paratroopers to Little Rock to protect the students, and placing the National Guard on federal service. During the entire academic year of 1957-1958 the paratroopers remained in Little Rock to protect the nine black students. Although Senator Richard Russell of Georgia likened the federal intervention in Little Rock to the tactics used by Hitler, events were moving against the segregationists. In 1959, Governor Faubus tried once more to stop integration by closing the high schools of Little Rock, but was eventually forced to reopen them when the Supreme Court overruled his actions in *Cooper v. Aaron* (1959). Little Rock could not resist the full force of the federal government.

Although the events at Little Rock are testimony to the problems which the Supreme Court faced when attempting to enforce its desegregation decisions, the importance of *Brown* should not be underestimated. By reversing the 'separate but equal' doctrine of *Plessy* the Court provided a lead and encouragement to black activists campaigning elsewhere for civil rights. In many ways the results of *Brown* were as evident in the Montgomery bus boycott of 1955-1956 as in the struggle at Little Rock. The boycott of the buses in Montgomery, Alabama began in December 1955 when a black woman, Rosa Parks, refused to give up her seat on a bus to a white man and was arrested. Under the aegis of the Montgomery Improvement Association the black community decided to organise a boycott of the buses as a protest against segregated seating on public transport in the city. Sustained by the charismatic leadership of the Reverend Dr Martin Luther King the boycott was extraordinarily successful. Blacks formed car pools, hitch-hiked, or simply walked. Victory was finally achieved when on 20 December 1956 the Supreme Court in the case *Gayle v. Browder* let stand a lower court ruling that segregated transportation was unconstitutional. The following day the Montgomery bus boycott came to an end.

The Montgomery bus boycott was important for two main reasons. First, it produced the group of black leaders who were to dominate the civil rights movement for the next decade. Immediately after the end of the boycott, Martin Luther King and a group of associates formed the Southern Christian Leadership Conference (SCLC) to co-ordinate future action. Second, the boycott helped to propel the issue of civil rights into national prominence. With television cameras covering both the events in Montgomery and the struggle to desegregate public schools in places like Little Rock, the pressure on Congress to act became irresistible. After a year's debate Congress finally passed the Civil Rights Act (1957). The first civil rights law passed by Congress since 1877, this measure established a Civil Rights Commission which was charged with investigating the denial of the voting rights of blacks in the South, and created a Civil Rights Division in the Justice Department which could seek court orders to prevent interference with the right to vote. One of the first actions of the Civil Rights

Commission was to report that the Civil Rights Act (1957) was ineffectual in protecting the voting rights of blacks. As a result Congress passed another measure. The Civil Rights Act (1960) empowered federal judges to appoint referees to register blacks where the court found a 'pattern and practice of discrimination'. Further, in an attempt to stop a spate of bomb attacks on buildings used by blacks, the Act also made it a federal crime to interfere with any court order or to transport explosives across a state line.

In dealing with the issue of civil rights the main problem facing President Eisenhower was to balance the legitimate demands of a particular group for a greater share of society's resources against the demands of other groups. Compounding the difficulties involved in this task was the fact that Eisenhower not only had to manage the ever-increasing demands for resources from domestic groups, but also had to deal with the consequences of the United States' emergence as a superpower following the Second World War. Some indication of the resources believed to be necessary to meet the country's new role in the world had already been indicated in the report *NSC-68* of the National Security Council (NSC) in 1950 which called for a vast increase in the military budget. Early in Eisenhower's second term a report to the NSC by the Security Resources Panel of the Science Advisory Council, known as the Gaither Report of September 1957, expressed similar sentiments. As in domestic policy, however, Eisenhower's intention was to reduce the level of government expenditure. He sought to offer what was termed a 'New Look' foreign and military policy. But just as his options in domestic affairs were limited by the legacy of the New Deal and Fair Deal, so his room for manoeuvre in foreign policy was restricted by the legacy of Yalta, the Marshall Plan, the Truman Doctrine and the Cold War. Throughout his administration, the United States' overseas commitments continued to multiply almost inexorably.

The negotiation of an armistice in Korea meant that the government no longer had to fund an expensive war. However, the general increase in the country's overseas commitments ensured that spending on defence remained high. They were unprecedented for peacetime. In 1929 federal expenditure on defence as a percentage of Gross National Product (GNP) stood for 1.7 per cent of GNP. In 1954 after the conclusion of the Korean war it stood at 12.9 per cent, but it declined steadily to 9.1 per cent of GNP by the end of Eisenhower's Administration. By 1959 approximately 41 per cent of the federal government's budget was devoted to defence. Whereas it had cost the federal government eighteen (1967) dollars to defend each American in 1929, by 1959 the government was spending 344 (1967) dollars to defend the same individual. Such per capita comparisons are, of course, a little unfair. By 1959 the United States not only had to defend Americans but also had to protect West Europeans, Southeast Asians, Israelis and numerous other nationalities. Superpower status did not come cheaply.

The direct and indirect consequences of the increase in defence spending during the 1950s were profound. Just as the New Deal had spawned a vast network of government agencies with close ties to various interest groups, so the increase in defence spending served to forge close relationships between the defence establishment and the defence industry. Government officials and business leaders co-operated with each other to promote an expansion of science-based industries. In this respect, the defence build-up of the 1950s put the final touches to the creation of the interest group state. Furthermore, because most of these industries were based in western and southern states like Texas and California, such developments did not only affect the structure of the federal government, but also contributed to the rise of the so-called Sunbelt. As traditional industries in the northern states declined, so people began migrating to the southern and western states in search of employment in the new defence industries. In the wake of economic and population growth came political power. Since the 1950s states in the south and west have steadily gained more seats in the US Congress and more electoral votes in presidential elections.

In his Farewell Address of 17 January 1961 Eisenhower warned the American people of some of the dangers posed by the 'Military–Industrial Complex'. Wary of the co-operative relationship which had emerged between the defence establishment and the defence industry he cautioned that 'In the councils of government, we must guard against the acquisition of unwarranted influence, whether sought or unsought, by the military–industrial complex'. He also expressed fears about the government's dominance of research and development: 'The prospect of domination of the nation's scholars by Federal employment, project allocations, and the power of money is ever present - and is gravely to be regarded'. Perhaps most prophetically, however, he also warned of the economic dangers of such high levels of defence spending:

As we peer into society's future, we – you and I, and our government – must avoid the impulse to live only for today, plundering, for our own ease and convenience, the precious resources of tomorrow. We cannot mortgage the material assets of our grandchildren without risking the loss also of their political and spiritual heritage. We want democracy to survive for all generations to come, not to become the insolvent phantom of tomorrow.

For although American democracy has survived, the economic cost of being a superpower has caused numerous problems.

On the surface the economic position of the United States during the 1950s appeared to be extremely healthy. Wartime devastation had destroyed the industries of the country's major economic competitors and left American industry to reap the benefits of a world anxious to rebuild itself, and a domestic population anxious to enjoy themselves after the frugalities of war. During the 1950s the United States led the world in economic growth. Its citizens enjoyed a rising per capita income, and unemployment averaged only 4.5 per cent compared with an average of 14.9 per cent between 1920 and 1939. For the average American, the 1950s were a time of plenty. Home ownership rose dramatically, and the new houses were filled with the very latest appliances: washing machines, vacuum cleaners and refrigerators. The term 'conspicuous consumption' took on real meaning as Americans rushed to buy the latest novelty. The suburbanite looked across the street and 'needed' what his neighbour possessed, whether it was the latest convertible or a swimming pool. Foreign travel, once the preserve of the rich and famous, became accessible to millions of Americans during the 1950s. For those who stayed at home, new tourist attractions like Disneyland were established. A new social group, the teenagers, were discovered and encouraged to spend their money on records, clothes and magazines. For many Americans, the 1950s truly seemed a time of affluence.

Among all the new consumer items that were to make their appearance in the 1950s, none was more pervasive than television. Found in only a few homes in 1950, the television soon came to dominate American life. Television transformed both patterns of family life, and the way in which politics was conducted. With the average American spending more hours each week watching television than working, the traditional social life of the nation was torn apart and established anew. The television dinner replaced the family meal. Forms of home entertainment were forgotten as millions sat down to watch shows such as 'I Love Lucy'. In the world of politics, the television commercial replaced the town meeting. The 'thirty second' television slot began to replace informed debate as politicians sought to exploit the new methods of communication. With the development of television, nothing would ever be quite the same again.

Beneath the images of economic success that were so common in the 1950s, however, lurked profound economic problems. Much of the rising standard of living enjoyed by Americans during the 1950s had been paid for through borrowing. Much of the 'affluence' of the 1950s had been facilitated by the twin inventions of the credit card and hire purchase. Consumer indebtedness stood at $196 billion in 1960. The result of such a splurge in consumption was a fall in the level of domestic investment. By 1960 total government and private investment in the United States as a percentage of GNP stood at 17.6 per cent, compared with 30.2 per cent in Japan and 24.3 per cent in West Germany. Of the major industrial nations of the West, only Britain had a lower rate of investment. To make matters worse, the United States' commitment to the free world ensured that dollars flowed abroad in the form of direct investment, foreign aid, or military assistance. Throughout the 1950s the capital account of the United States was almost continuously in the red. In other words, the United States was sending more money abroad in the form of investment and other capital flows than it was taking in. As Eisenhower had warned, the country's commitments as a superpower had caused it to mortgage its future.

The economic consequences of the United States' emergence as a superpower were not readily apparent in 1960. Questions about how the country could continue to commit vast resources to defence, and satisfy the increasing demands of the American population, while the economy declined, were not yet being asked. It would take the traumatic events of the 1960s, together with a stagflating economy, to bring them into sharp focus. In 1960 the electorate of the United States simply wanted a change. Rejecting the cautious approach of the 1950s they turned to a young, energetic man to usher in the 1960s. John F. Kennedy held up to the American people a vision of what government could achieve. It was a vision they were ready to accept.

Further reading

Stephen E. Ambrose, *Eisenhower*, 2 vols. (New York, 1983, 1984).

Michael R. Beschloss, *Eisenhower* (New York, 1990).

Fred Greenstein, *The Hidden-Hand Presidency: Eisenhower as Leader* (New York, 1982).

J. Ronald Oakley, *God's Country: America in the Fifties* (New York, 1986).

Herbert S. Parmet, *Eisenhower and the American Crusade* (New York, 1972).

James L. Sundquist, *Politics and Policy* (Washington D. C., 1968).

7

Foreign policy in the Eisenhower era, 1953-1960

Americans who supported General Dwight Eisenhower, or 'Ike' as he was affectionately known, for President in the 1952 election voted for him for two reasons: it was time for a change and they trusted him. He had an instinctive grasp of public relations, he was good company, he projected a sense of self-confidence and he believed that differences between individuals could be resolved by common sense, good will and visible decency. While these qualities would undoubtedly serve him well in his capacity as head of the government, they would not necessarily equip him in his conduct of foreign affairs, particularly with the Soviets. Although Stalin only lived for a few weeks after the inauguration – he died on 5 March, 1953 – there was no certainty that his successors would alter the direction of Soviet foreign policy. So even if the personality of the new President was different, there could be no immediate change of course. Like the architects of containment, Eisenhower believed that the Soviet Union was expansionist, and that ideology was just the instrument of expansion. He detested communism, but he could live with it as long as it did not intrude on American interests. He felt that there was no ultimate reason why nations could not live in harmony just as different interest groups do within a nation. As a former soldier he believed in the deterrent value of a strong military defence. He never contemplated the destruction of the communist enemy by means of war, in Asia or anywhere else. He sought the prevention of change through the absolute assurance that aggression would be countered by the full military might of the United States.

He left the articulation of policy to his Secretary of State, John Foster Dulles, who combined his considerable knowledge of international affairs with his skill in adversarial procedure acquired as a corporation lawyer. Like all good lawyers he liked a good fight. Dulles believed that the fibre of the nation could be best preserved by accepting challenges, by moving into the fray and meeting threats head-on. He agreed with Eisenhower that the new administration could not act more forcefully than its predecessor; but it could speak more forcefully. Dulles would use fighting words. Words would mobilize the nation and hide the fact that the deeds of Eisenhower's Administration were not substantially different to those of Truman's. Dulles also knew that the Republican party had a vocal and powerful anti-communist right wing. He did not sympathize with it, but he was aware that its views had to be reflected in his policies. He would be its spokesman, even if he did not care that much for its sentiments. His ethical posturing was undertaken for political purposes. He was sufficiently intelligent and experienced to realize that the world was more complex than his utterances admitted. Tough talk was not diplomacy. But that was not the point. Dulles' rhetoric must be seen as a public relations exercise. A full understanding of the foreign policy of the Eisenhower years can only be gleaned by examining the statesmanship of the President in conjunction with the rhetoric of his Secretary of State.

President Eisenhower did not have any consuming sense of dissatisfaction with containment. Indeed, as NATO Supreme Commander he had been responsible for implementing Truman's European policy. But he believed, as did John Foster Dulles, that the United States could achieve greater effectiveness at less cost by placing more emphasis on the deterrent value of nuclear weapons. The United States' opponents should not take it for granted that the United States would just wage limited war in disputes that were not of central concern to it. Dulles in particular wanted it known that nuclear weapons would not be weapons of last resort, but plausible instruments of diplomacy. The United States would not be afraid to use them first. According to Dulles, the trouble with containment was that it froze the balance of power. Frontiers, alliances and relations between states were not hermetically sealed. Things change. On several occasions Dulles called for the eventual 'liberation' of the Soviet satellites, though this was a statement of aspiration rather than of realistic expectation. But despite such talk of 'rollback' and 'liberation' the new Eisenhower Administration continued more than it changed. It accepted the strategy of containing Soviet power despite frequent dismissals of the policy as a negative exercise. If anything brought the two men together, it was hope rather than immediate intellectual affinity.

When the new administration came into office, most Republicans,

Eisenhower included, believed that Truman's defence policies threatened national bankruptcy. The nation could not afford expanded
nuclear and conventional forces. They were in constant search for that
holiest of grails, the balanced budget. The New Look, as their defence
strategy was dubbed, with its reliance on nuclear weapons and its
insistence on the acceptability of their use as a theatre weapon, was
developed in part to cut down on more expensive conventional
weapons. According to the Republicans, the Truman Administration
had ignored the economic strain that a massive rearmament programme would impose. The architects of the New Look assumed that
a serious military engagement would soon go nuclear, so a large
conventional force was unnecessary. They also hoped that with such
large destructive power at their command they could control or
thwart unwanted change in most areas of the globe. The Secretary of
the Treasury, George Humphrey, believed that the National Security
Council should concentrate on what it could afford in its defence
planning. Eisnhower sympathized with the desire to cut back costs.
Military defence should be adequate but not excessive. He did not
believe that the economy should come to depend on defence expenditure. He feared for the consequences on the free economy and
warned about building a garrison state. 'It is perfectly clear,' he told
a group of legislative leaders in 1959, 'that you can't provide security
with a checkbook ... Any one who has read a little bit on Communism
... knows that the Communist objective is to make us spend ourselves
into bankruptcy.' The new President seemed to be more sceptical than
his immediate advisers, particularly Dulles, about automatically invok-
ing American military power. He was as much the cold warrior, but he
was more aware of the political and international constraints on
national security policy. While he did not hesitate to use the threat of
nuclear war whenever he thought it necessary, he generally maintained
a calm and thoughtful approach to foreign policy. But he wanted his
adversaries to know that that the United States would respond to
provocation and that that response would take any form, including the
use of atomic weapons. 'The ability to get to the verge without getting
into the war is the necessary art,' Dulles told *Life* magazine in 1956.
While Truman's containment policy sought to inject an element of
certainty into American policy, Eisenhower wanted to keep the other
side guessing.

The apparent willingness to use nuclear weapons was most clearly
illustrated in the administration's Asian policies. His first task as

President was to end the Korean war, which was deadlocked on the field and in the negotiations. He wanted an honorable peace; he was not interested in taking the odd hill or a few miles of territory. When the stalemate in the negotiations, particularly over the repatriation of prisoners-of-war, continued, the President let it be known to the Chinese that he 'would not be limited by any world-wide gentleman's agreement' to keep the war on its current path. He would use Chinese Nationalist troops and 'move decisively without inhibition in our use of weapons.' The Chinese knew he would not allow the conflict to go on any longer. Eisenhower was new to office and was staking his reputation. The Chinese responded and on 27 July 1953 an armistice agreement was signed. The long and increasingly unpopular war had come to an end.

But though peace had come to Korea, the United States found itself increasingly involved in Asian affairs. In Indochina war between the the communist-dominated Vietminh under the leadership of Ho Chi Minh and their colonial French masters had been raging ever since France had re-established its rule there after the defeat of Japan in 1945. When hostilities had broken out in Korea, President Truman committed himself to aiding the French effort, and by 1954 the United States was paying over three quarters of the cost of the French campaign. The United States financed the war because it wanted France to meet its NATO obligations and because in its view Indochina was crucial to the strategic balance. It had vital raw materials; its people, according to the Americans, did not want to live under communist rule. Above all, if Indochina became communist there would be an unstoppable contagion. Eisenhower called this the ' 'falling domino' principle. You have a row of dominoes set up,' he explained, 'you knock over the first one, and what will happen to the last one is the certainty that it will go over very quickly.' He wanted a French victory, but not at any price. If his staunch anti-communist stance was to have credibility, the United States would have to act. The Republicans had made political capital out of accusations as to who 'lost' China. They did not particularly want to lose Vietnam. Eisenhower equally did not want American troops to be bogged down in yet another Asian war. But the pressure for intervention was building up. When communist forces tightened the noose by surrounding the main French fortress at Dienbienphu it became clear that without outside military assistance the French cause was hopeless. Eisenhower was prepared to consider intervention, but only if he received unequivocal political and international support. He mooted joint action with the British, but Churchill would have none of it. And he had a foresight that President Johnson, a decade later, would sadly not possess. The jungles of Indochina, he said, would swallow division after division; and there would be no thanks. A western intervention would only be resented by the local populace which wanted to get the fighting over with and live in peace. Eisenhower was finally convinced that an intervention was unthinkable when he failed, much to his relief, to secure congressional support for an air strike. On 29 April 1954 the National Security Council formally resolved to postpone action and a week later the French defenders surrendered.

The western powers tried to salvage their influence in the peace talks being held at at Geneva. They did quite well. Under the agreed Geneva Accords, Vietnam was partitioned pending fresh elections; Cambodia and Laos were given independent status. The Americans took over responsibility from France in the area and became the protector of the southern part of Vietnam. Laos and Cambodia were granted the explicit right of self-defence. Both Dulles and Eisenhower were confident that the removal of the French complication would create an opportunity for the United States to build a viable non-communist alternative in South-East Asia. They believed that alliances could be nurtured and managed. Dulles signed up interested allies, including France and Britain, for the South-East Asia Treaty Organization (SEATO) by which the signatories bound themselves to defend the 'peace and security' of the region. The National Security Council resolved 'to maintain a friendly non-communist South Vietnam and to prevent a Communist victory through all-Vietnam elections'. South Vietnam was to become the great laboratory in American nation-building. But there was not going to be democracy at any price. The administration firmly backed its client, Ngo Dinh Diem, the premier of South Vietnam, in his decision to block the elections that could have opened the way for reunification as provided by the Geneva accords. Neither party had any serious interest in reunification and soon the seventeenth parallel became one of the most rigid frontiers in the world. Thus while Eisenhower's caution had resulted in the 'loss' of North Vietnam, he did gain a new regional collective security organization and, in South Vietnam, a client that would become the great bastion of American influence in the decade to come.

While Dulles was in Manila presiding over the birth of SEATO another crisis in the Far East broke out, this time in the small islands

off the shore of mainland China that were still in the hands of the
Chiang Kai-shek government in Taiwan (Formosa). The tiny islands
of Quemoy and the Matsu chain to the North were possible stepping
stones for a mainland communist invasion of Taiwan or, conversely,
but rather less likely in practice, a Nationalist invasion (or re-occupa-
tion) of the mainland. The Communists resented the Nationalist
presence on their doorstep, particularly as commando raids were
occasionally carried out from the islands. So in September 1954 the
forces of the People's Republic began shelling Quemoy from batteries
on the shore line. Eisenhower responded firmly, but showed he was
willing to compromise. He made treaty arrangements for the defence
of Taiwan and pledged support of 'closely related localities'. He
yielded a little when he ordered American ships to help the Nationalists evacuate the Tachen islands to the north of the Matsu chain. But
he appeared to dig in his heels on the issue of Quemoy and Matsu. In
March 1955 the President replied to a reporter's question on the
offshore islands: 'Now, in any combat where these things [atomic
weapons] can be used on strictly military targets and for strictly
military purposes, I see no reason why they shouldn't be used just
exactly as you would use a bullet or anything else.' Eisenhower's
rather casual comparison of atomic weapons to bullets set off a war
scare. It is doubtful whether Eisenhower really envisaged using
weapons on an area that was clearly not of central significance to
American security. He did not even contemplate sending ground
troops to Taiwan. But the Chinese feared he meant business. Talks
commenced, and while nothing was resolved, the shelling stopped.
Something of a re-run occurred in the summer of 1958; once more
there were veiled threats of nuclear escalation, but in private the
President advocated restraint. He had invoked the idea of massive
retaliation, but kept the Chinese guessing as to whether it would apply
to the offshore islands. While his invocation of atomic bombs was
perhaps cavalier – and he never even tried to appreciate that the
Chinese Communists saw Chiang's stronghold just off the coast as an
affront to national pride – he emerged from the crisis with all his
objectives intact. The American commitment to Taiwan was stronger
than ever, he had re-established his credentials with the China Lobby
at home and he kept the peace without losing ground. As in the
resolution of the Indochina crisis, he had never foreclosed his options.
Although subsequent presidents did not threaten the use of the
ultimate weapon as readily as Eisenhower, they did not learn that

particular lesson.

Eisenhower's reluctance to make specific public commitments was something of a hallmark. Eisenhower did not like to issue public threats or promises unless he thought there was a good chance they would be heeded. He liked to deliver. One effective way of intervening abroad without making commitments that might be difficult to fulfil was by subterfuge and the use of secret operations. Clandestine activities permitted the United States to disclaim any responsibilty for actions that the administration either did not want to be attributed to it or to save face in the event that its plots backfired. The Central Intelligence Agency (CIA) had been authorized to carry out special operations since 1948, but they did not really come into their own until the Eisenhower years. During the 1950s the CIA conducted guerilla operations in North Vietnam, organized aerial reconnaissance missions over China and the Soviet Union, and considered assassination attempts on a number of foreign leaders including Fidel Castro of Cuba and Patrice Lumumba of the Congo. More significantly, it successfully organized the overthrow of two foreign governments, that of Iran in 1953 and of Guatemala in 1954. In Iran Eisenhower authorized the CIA to engineer a political coup when its nationalist prime minister, Mohammed Mossadeq, nationalized the oil fields formerly owned by the Anglo-Iranian Oil Company (now BP). This was followed by a western boycott of Iranian oil. Partly in retaliation Mossadeq received a Soviet aid mission and extended a hand to the Iranian communist party. The CIA gave Kermit Roosevelt, a grandson of Theodore Roosevelt, overall responsibility for the coup. He recruited a street mob with the help of the Iranian police, organized street demonstrations, forced the capitulation of Mossadeq and brought the Shah back from exile as absolute ruler of Iran. The new government formed a new oil consortium and was immediately recognized by the United States and assisted with economic aid.

In Guatemala the CIA's intervention was more overt. When the democratically elected government of Jacobo Arbenz began its programme of land reform, Eisenhower decided that the reforms, which included the nationalization of idle acreage belonging to the American-owned United Fruit Company, constituted a threat. The advice he received was hastily conceived at best and tainted with financial self-interest at worst. Eisenhower genuinely believed that Arbenz was a communist and that he would establish a Soviet foothold in Latin America; so he gave the go-ahead for another coup. The CIA picked

Castillo Armas to lead the insurrection. In June 1954 Armas invaded Guatemala City with a small force of men trained in Honduras and supported by CIA pilots based in Managua. Arbenz fled and was replaced by a military dictatorship that banned all opposition parties and reversed the land reforms of the Arbenz government. The United States' somewhat ignominious involvement was consistent with its traditional policy of keeping order by whatever means in its own back yard. The episode revealed once again Eisenhower's propensity to take risks, though he limited those risks by minimizing or concealing the extent of the American involvement.

Guatemala and Iran were still sideshows. Since the late 1930s the United States had directly exercised its power in its major areas of interest in Europe, the Far East and Latin America. In the Middle East it had relied on British and French power to ensure stability. But as Anglo-French colonialism and hegemony were challenged by the rising tide of nationalism, the United States felt the need to distance itself from the Europeans and sought to find a way of preventing the area from becoming embroiled in the Cold War. The valuable oil resources were a crucial prize. It began by forming with Britain the Baghdad Pact, a defensive alliance with Turkey, Iran, Pakistan and Iraq. It then offered financial help to President Gamel Abdel Nasser of Egypt for his ambitious Aswan Dam project on the Nile. But the deal was scotched when the Egyptians, eager to keep a foot in both camps, recognized communist China and made an arms deal with the Czechs. Deprived of outside finance and eager to boost his credentials as a nationalist, Nasser nationalized the Suez Canal, whose stock was jointly held by Britain and France. The British and French were furious; a valuable asset had been seized, a strategically vital area was cut off and Nasser had set himself up as a model to the rest of the Arab world which was still trying to divest itself of the shackles of colonialism. Anthony Eden, the British Prime Minister, and Guy Mollet, Prime Minister of France, plotted to bring down Nasser. They entered into secret negotiations with the Israelis who also wanted to see an end to the regime that had harboured Arab terrorists and had openly called for the overthrow of the Jewish state. They agreed on a cunning but disastrous joint invasion plan. The Israelis would invade to the south in the Sinai desert; the British and French after a pre-arranged ultimatum to both sides would send in troops to seize the Suez canal.

When the invasion materialized and was shortly followed by bombing on 31 October Eisenhower was furious. He had been taken totally by surprise. The United States' closest allies had been as secretive as the Japanese before Pearl Harbor. The Anglo-French invasion, begun five days later, smacked of Victorian colonialism (the President conveniently forgot his own similar action in Guatemala) and, worse, provided an excuse for the Soviet Union to enter the region in the role of protector. Dulles was equally gloomy: a good opportunity to exploit Soviet repression in Eastern Europe had been lost. How could the United States react to the cruel invasion of Hungary when its own NATO allies were colluding to topple regimes they did not like? Nevertheless, he placed the army on a full alert, while exerting utmost pressure on Britain and France to accept the cease-fire resolutions of the United Nations. And he warned them that the United States would not make good the shortfall of oil that had arisen as a result of the closure of the canal. Deprived of oil, Britain and France were forced to withdraw. With their retreat an entire era had come to an end.

The United States recognized there were now new configurations of power. In January 1957 Eisenhower asked Congress for an economic and military assistance programme for the Middle East and for a general authority to use armed force to protect nations who asked for aid against 'overt armed aggression from any nation controlled by International Communism'. While the President was correct in thinking that the Suez crisis had drawn the Soviets into an area in which its influence had until then been slight, his 'Eisenhower Doctrine', as it came to be called, was something of a red herring. True, it was Eisenhower's intention to make the American commitment unambiguous and to heal the wounds with Britain and France. However, the main threat to the independence of pro-western nations, as subsequent events in Jordan and Lebanon were to show, came from Arab nationalism. And if the Soviets did penetrate a particular country, that country was hardly likely to ask for American aid. Indeed it almost invited the Soviets to step up their activities in the area. The Eisenhower Doctrine was not consistent with the President's rather successful formula of keeping the adversary guessing. Vagueness is often more effective, if only because it gives flexibility.

One particularly infuriating aspect of the entire Suez crisis was that it tended to overshadow the traumatic events unfolding in Hungary. Encouraged by the repudiation of Stalinism, Hungarians were demanding greater political and intellectual freedoms. After pro-democracy riots, a new premier, Imre Nagy, was installed to head the government in Budapest. The riots did not stop and the Soviet Union sent in troops to restore order and quash the drift to autonomy. Hungarian freedom fighters began to throw home-made bombs at the invading tanks; some Hungarian soldiers even defected. There was nothing the Eisenhower Administration could do, particularly as the Suez crisis was about to burst on to the scene. But the administration's caution invited criticism fom those who wondered what John Dulles' calls for 'liberation' of the Soviet satellites had been all about. The Hungarians reminded the United States of their many references over the years to liberation in speeches and radio broadcasts, but Eisenhower knew there was no way he could challenge the Soviets so close to their border.

Despite Eisenhower's low esteem for the Soviet regime, he always looked to the possibilities for easing tensions with the Soviet Union. The pursuit of a more lasting peace became the principal driving force of his presidency. He never relinquished his belief that the balance of political and military power had to be maintained, but he felt that unless he was seen to be 'waging peace' (the title of one volume of his memoirs) his tenure of office would be a failure. He sincerely believed that if he could convince the new Soviet leadership of Nikita Khrushchev and Nikolai Bulganin that the United States wished them no harm, he could persuade them to accept western solutions for arms control, European security and international economic development. Conditions seemed right for a fresh approach. Stalin was dead and within the Soviet Union the process of repudiation of the Stalinist era was already under way. In the United States Senator Joseph McCarthy, the communist witch-hunter, had destroyed himself by his own excesses, and there was less mileage to be had from indiscriminate antagonism to communism. Peace had come to Korea. Both superpowers had completed their own security arrangements. The United States had drawn up a series of alliances in Australasia, the Middle East and the Far East, and on the European front West Germany had joined NATO. The Soviet Union had concluded its own series of agreements, culminating in May 1955 in the Treaty of Friendship, Co-operation and Mutual Assistance (the Warsaw Pact). While these security arrangements confirmed the division of Europe, they acknowledged the political and military realities of the Cold War. These treaties helped each side to convince itself that it was in a position to explore peace, since it was negotiating from a position of strength.

For this reason hopes were high when the President travelled to

Geneva in July 1955 for his first summit conference with the Soviets. By and large the conference was relaxed and saw some patient diplomacy, although there were no agreements on anything of importance. Eisenhower launched one of his many initiatives in the field of arms control. He proposed his pet scheme for 'open skies'; this involved an exchange of information about the size and whereabouts of each nation's military forces, backed by the automatic right of aerial reconnaissance to check up on the facts. The Soviet Union rejected the proposal out of hand. In their view it violated their territorial integrity and would give them little information that they did not already possess. Eisenhower sincerely believed that his scheme would generate mutual trust and open the opportunity for further arms inspection systems. He did not really grasp that the Soviets were being asked to give away more than they were getting. In western eyes Eisenhower had enhanced his reputation as a peace-maker. Further attempts at bridging the chasm were temporarily dashed by the Suez and Hungarian crises. These events worsened relations; each side accused the other of perfidy and expansionism. But as Eisenhower noted in his memoirs, the 'spirit of Geneva' never faded entirely. Indeed the way was opened for some increase in intercourse between East and West. Above all, in Dulles' words, Geneva had generated 'a confirmation of the joint commitment to avoid nuclear war'. Eisenhower continued to devote much of his personal energy to finding means of reducing the danger of nuclear war. He instructed the Atomic Energy Commission to keep weapons testing to a minimum, in part to quell the mounting tide of concern about the impact of nuclear fall-out. He pursued his dream of a treaty with the Soviets banning all nuclear tests, but hope was dashed when the Soviets launched the first earth satellite, *Sputnik*. The Soviet achievement produced a near-hysterical reaction in the United States. The press and politicians lost their self-confidence. Americans had assumed since 1945 that they were the best educated and the most technologically advanced society in the world. Now it seemed the Soviets had the edge. The fear was raised that *Sputnik* was the first step in the development of space-launched nuclear warheads. The administration's contention that it was still ahead in the race to deliver intercontinental ballistic missiles was not believed. *Sputnik* stimulated calls for large increases in spending on missile research, weapons and fall-out shelters. *Sputnik* also had one therapeutic effect: by making Americans look to their own scientific and educational achievements it deflected the crudest vestiges of McCarthyism. The Soviets' scientific triumph was not ascribed to disloyalty and treachery within the United States but to the quality of American scientific education. However, this panic made an arms control agreement less acceptable. If people believed that the Soviets were ahead, they would not favour a freeze on weapons development and testing.

Eisenhower's position was made even more difficult when the Soviets announced in March 1958 that they would suspend further nuclear testing. The Soviets had just completed their current series of tests, and the halt was convenient. This was embarrassing for the administration which was about to begin a new test series, code-named HARDTACK. Eisenhower still gave the go-ahead, but persuaded the Soviets to begin negiotiations on a test ban and an international control system in Geneva in October 1958. Both sides squeezed in as many tests as possible before the conference but afterwards there were no more significant atmospheric tests for three years. Eisenhower's unilateral moratorium – the Soviets had followed suit – won worldwide approval, particularly as the harmful effects of fall-out became more widely known. He became increasingly consumed by his mission to improve relations between the two superpowers, particularly after Dulles' death on 24 May 1959. He invited Khrushchev to visit the United States and meet privately with him. Khrushchev accepted; he also wanted peace. But to the Soviet peace meant not just a curb on weapons testing. He wanted to keep nuclear weapons out of Germany and to prevent their further proliferation in Europe. Indeed, earlier in November he had precipitated another crisis in Berlin on this very issue. The Soviets could not disentangle the issue of arms control from the rearmament of Germany. A blockade and a threat of world war over Berlin would, Khrushchev hoped, make Eisenhower more tractable over the issue of German rearmament in particular and arms control in general. Khrushchev came to America in September 1959. The two leaders got on. Eisenhower took him for a helicopter ride in the hope of impressing the Soviet with American affluence. Khrushchev was not impressed; the sight of all those traffic jams persuaded him that the Americans were too restless and their cars were wasteful. At their meeting at Camp David which marked the climax of the visit, the two leaders agreed to meet again at a summit in May 1960 in Paris. Khrushchev removed the deadline on his plan to sign a separate peace treaty with East Germany, so terminating Allied rights in Berlin. Determined to keep up the initiative on arms reduction Khrushchev also proposed to the Supreme Soviet that the Red Army should be reduced from 3.6 million men to 2.4 million, a cut of one-third. He said it could be done unilaterally and without harm to Soviet security. It seemed that the Soviets were making most of the moves in reducing East–West tensions. The administration could offer no counter-proposal; in its view NATO's conventional forces had been pared down to the bare minimum. It wanted to focus on nuclear weapons.

The Paris summit was perhaps doomed to failure. There had been no breakthrough in the Geneva arms talks and Khrushchev's threat to terminate all occupation rights in Berlin still loomed. Within his own ranks Khrushchev faced mounting criticism: his proposals for force reductions in the East were criticized by hardliners in the Politburo and the negotiations on disarmament and the test ban received a hostile reception from the Soviet Union's Chinese neighbours. By May 1960 Khrushchev feared that an agreement with the West could undermine the Soviet Union's stature among the world's communist parties. Eisenhower gave Khrushchev the perfect excuse to retrace his steps. On 1 May 1960 an American U2 reconnaissance aircraft, which could take secret photographs from high altitude, was shot down over Soviet territory. A week later Khrushchev stunned the world by announcing the downing of the aircraft and the capture, alive, of its pilot Gary Powers. Eisenhower had to admit responsibility; failure to do so would have been an admission that he was not in control of policy. He admitted he had fallen into a trap, but proclaimed that spying 'is a distasteful but vital necessity'. Khrushchev's outrage was somewhat hypocritical – he had prided himself on the Soviet Union's achievements in the field of reconnaissance. He still insisted on a personal apology and a specific renunciation of spy flights but Eisenhower had no intention of giving him one. They went to Paris for the theatrical showdown. The Soviet leader launched into a vitriolic tirade against the United States, withdrew his invitation for Eisenhower to visit Moscow and promptly stalked out. The summit was over before it started.

It was not just the Paris summit that was over. Eisenhower believed that his poor judgement in permitting the continuation of the U2 flights had not just aborted a summit, but it had ruined the prospect of a test ban treaty and, who knows, a wider arms control agreement. Eisenhower's vitality was sapped after Paris. If his major goal had been to end the Cold War, then he had indeed fluffed it. The truth of the matter was that both men had allowed their anger and their pride to overshadow their aspirations. But Eisenhower did have achievements in foreign policy to his name. His strategy of deterrence had worked when it had been invoked. He had increased the nation's nuclear stockpiles: they had trebled in the two years between 1958 and 1960. He had reduced the proportion of the federal budget spent on defence without endangering the national security. He had ended a military conflict in Korea and had wisely avoided one in Indochina by standing firm against some of his closest advisers. Despite his frequent warnings of the growing power of the military and industry he had remained in control, and had used that control to take peace initiatives that would have been unthinkable at the beginning of the decade.

Further reading

Stephen E. Ambrose, *Eisenhower, the President: 1952-1969* (London, 1984).

H. W. Brands, *Cold Warriors: Eisenhower's Generation and American Foreign Policy* (New York, 1988).

Robert A. Divine, *Eisenhower and the Cold War* (New York, 1981).

John L. Gaddis, *Strategies of Containment: A Critical Appraisal of Postwar National Security Policy* (New York, 1982).

Michael Guhin, *John Foster Dulles: A Statesman and His Times* (New York, 1972).

Norman A. Graebner (ed.), *The National Security: Its Theory and Practice* (New York and Oxford, 1986).

Townsend Hoopes, *The Devil and John Foster Dulles* (Boston, 1973).

8

Towards a Great Society, 1961-1968

Although the 1950s had brought a rising standard of living to many Americans, the apparent complacency of the Eisenhower Administration had begun to cause considerable disquiet by the end of the decade. Fuelled by an optimism born of prosperity, expectations about what the government could achieve rose steadily. Eminent social scientists, such as J. K. Galbraith, captured the spirit of the time by suggesting that the social environment could be manipulated to produce certain results in the same way that scientists had shown that the material world could be manipulated to man's advantage. The prevailing sentiment was that there was little that government could not do if only greater courage and leadership were to be shown.

The man who was to benefit most from the growing conviction that the country needed a more forceful leader was Senator John F. Kennedy, a Democrat from Massachusetts. Despite an undistinguished record in the Senate, Kennedy managed to secure the Democratic nomination for President in 1960 through a combination of family wealth and political acumen. At the Democratic Party's Convention in Los Angeles, Kennedy offered a vision of the future that was both exciting and vague. In his acceptance speech he declared: 'We stand today on the edge of a New Frontier - the frontier of unknown opportunities and perils - a frontier of unfulfilled hopes and threats.' Kennedy's rhetoric seemed to promise a period of change and unlimited possibilities.

Senator Kennedy's opponent in the general election was Vice-President Richard M. Nixon. Nixon was well-known and a skilled politician, but his campaign was hindered by his association with the Eisenhower Administration. With the electorate looking for a leader who offered change, Nixon's links with the past were a liability. In the event, the election of 1960 was the closest presidential election since 1888 with Kennedy gaining a mere 118,574 popular votes more than

Nixon. The electoral college vote was more decisive with Kennedy winning 303 votes and Nixon 219 votes.

In keeping with his carefully crafted image of dynamic leadership, Kennedy filled his cabinet with young and intelligent people. Most notably, Robert S. McNamara was appointed Secretary of Defense, McGeorge Bundy was made National Security Advisor, and Robert F. Kennedy, his younger brother, was chosen as Attorney-General. For all of the accent on youth, change and new opportunities, however, Kennedy had few concrete policy proposals. The 'New Frontier' of his acceptance speech was to all intents and purposes empty rhetoric. Neither were any specific policy goals articulated in Kennedy's Inaugural Address of 20 January 1961. Rather than detailing a policy programme, Kennedy used the occasion to deliver a speech of soaring rhetoric. 'Let the word go forth from this time and place,' he declared, 'Let every nation know, whether it wishes us well or ill, that we shall pay any price, hear any burden, meet any hardship, support any friend, oppose any foe, to assure the survival and success of liberty. And so, my fellow Americans: ask not what your country can do for you - ask what you can do for your country.' As with so much of the Kennedy era, the accent was on style rather than substance.

The lack of a clear, coherent programme hindered Kennedy when it came to securing the passage of legislation through Congress. Suggested on a piecemeal basis, Kennedy's legislative proposals were easily blocked by conservatives in Congress. Between 1961 and 1963, Congress blocked efforts to provide health insurance for the elderly, increase federal aid to education, reform the tax system and create a Department of Urban Affairs. Perhaps most seriously, Kennedy never understood the importance of the civil rights movement. Although he occasionally made dramatic gestures of support for civil rights leaders, he was also responsible for ordering the Federal Bureau of Investigations (FBI) to tap the telephone of Martin Luther King.

The struggle for civil rights was to dominate domestic politics in the United States during the early 1960s. On 1 February 1960 the philosophy of non-violent resistance, which had characterized the civil rights movement since the Montgomery bus boycott of 1956, took on a new form when four black students from North Carolina Agricultural and Technical College sat at the 'whites only' lunch counter of the Woolworths store in Greensboro, North Carolina. The following day about 30 students joined the 'sit-in'. On Wednesday, 3 February, over 50 black students and 3 white students returned to Woolworths to continue the demonstration. By the end of the week the store was forced to close its doors to the public. News of this form of non-violent resistance spread rapidly, first across North Carolina, and then across other southern states. Within a week, sit-ins were being staged in other North Carolina cities. By the end of February black students were holding sit-ins in cities such as Richmond, Virginia, Baltimore, Maryland, and Nashville, Tennessee. In other cities, the sit-ins became 'stand-ins' at theatres, 'wade-ins' at swimming pools or beaches and 'kneel-ins' at churches. Faced with demonstrations on such a large scale, some cities agreed to change their discriminatory laws. Whites in other cities, however, responded more violently to the challenge presented by the new form of non-violent resistance. Non-violent black protestors were attacked with knives and clubs and burned with cigarettes.

The climax of the struggle for civil rights was to occur in 1963. In April 1963 a campaign of direct action by the civil rights movement was begun in Birmingham, Alabama. On 3 April 1963 a number of black activists began a series of sit-ins in various Birmingham stores. Eight days later, Martin Luther King was arrested as he led a march through the city. Over the following few weeks Police Commissioner Eugene 'Bull' Connor authorized the use of tear gas, attack dogs, electric cattle prods and fire hoses to disperse peaceful protestors. With millions of Americans watching the events in Birmingham on television, pressure rapidly mounted for the federal government to intervene. Overcoming a reluctance to become involved in the affairs of Alabama, President Kennedy finally sent Burke Marshall, head of the Civil Rights Division of the Justice Department, to Birmingham on 4 May 1963. On 10 May 1963, Marshall reached an agreement with the white leaders of the city which ended the campaign. The agreement included terms providing for local hiring policies on a 'nondiscriminatory' basis and the immediate release of all those arrested during the campaign.

To take advantage of the publicity generated by the campaign in Birmingham, Alabama, the leaders of the civil rights movement organized a 'March on Washington'. On 28 August 1963, a biracial crowd of over 200,000 people marched down the Mall in Washington DC towards the Lincoln Memorial. Assembled in front of the Memorial the crowd listened to speeches from a number of civil rights leaders. It was a speech by Martin Luther King, however, which dominated the day's proceedings. Departing from his prepared text,

King informed the crowd that:

> ... I still have a dream. It is a dream deeply rooted in the American Dream.
> I have a dream that one day this nation will rise up and live out the true
> meaning of its creed - we hold these truths to be self-evident, that all men
> are created equal.

After elaborating upon his 'Dream', King concluded that:

> When we allow freedom to ring ... we will be able to speed up that day
> when all of God's children - black men and white men, Jews and Gentiles,
> Protestants and Catholics - will be able to join hands and sing in the words
> of the old Negro spiritual, 'Free at last, free at last; thank God Almighty,
> we are free at last'.

By setting the struggle for civil rights against the promises of the
Declaration of Independence, the 'I Have a Dream' speech affirmed
the moral authority of the civil rights movement before a television
audience of millions. In this way King managed to convey the justice
of his cause to those white Americans who had no experience of
conditions in the South.

The pressure for federal action to guarantee the civil rights of black
Americans grew inexorably in the aftermath of the 'March on Wash-
ington'. Passage of a civil rights bill that had been sponsored by
President Kennedy, however, seemed unlikely given the hostility of
southern Democrats in the US Senate. Only the assassination of
President Kennedy on 22 November 1963, and President Lyndon B.
Johnson's subsequent plea for the passage of the bill as a memorial to
the slain President, overcame southern resistance to the measure.
Signed into law on 2 July 1964, the Civil Rights Act (1964) was the
most important civil rights measure ever to be passed by Congress.
The Act prohibited discrimination in public accommodations and
employment, defined the literacy requirements for voting and empowered the Attorney-General to bring suits to desegregate schools.
The Act also created an Equal Employment Opportunity Commission
to administer the ban on discrimination in employment practices.

For all of the wide-ranging provisions of the Civil Rights Act
(1964), the measure failed to guarantee the black population in the
South the right to vote. A move in this direction had been made with
the ratification of the 24th Amendment in 1964 which abolished the
poll tax. Prior to the ratification of the 24th Amendment several states
had imposed a tax on voting to deny poor blacks the franchise.
Although the 24th Amendment removed one obstacle to the black

population's exercise of the franchise, events at Selma, Alabama, where a march organized by the civil rights movement was violently broken up by police on 7 March 1965, provided an indication that voting rights needed to be further protected. The result was the passage of the Voting Rights Act (1965) which President Johnson signed into law on 6 August 1965. The Voting Rights Act (1965) abolished literacy tests and other barriers which had been used to prevent blacks from voting. It also empowered the Attorney-General to dispatch federal examiners to register voters in states or counties where fewer than half the population had voted in 1964.

The Civil Rights Act (1964) and the Voting Rights Act (1965) were part of a torrent of legislation that would be enacted by Congress in the years immediately following Kennedy's assassination in Dallas, Texas. When Kennedy was shot by Lee Harvey Oswald, he was succeeded as President by Vice-President Lyndon B. Johnson. A greater difference in style between two men would be difficult to imagine. Whereas Kennedy was charming, even charismatic, Johnson was often brusque to the point of being rude. What Johnson possessed that Kennedy lacked, however, was a deep concern for the disadvantaged within society and the leadership skills necessary to advance his agenda through Congress. That agenda comprised nothing less than almost the entire compass of twentieth-century liberalism.

An indication of the scope of President Johnson's agenda was given in his first State of the Union message on 8 January 1964. Johnson told the assembled members of Congress that: 'Unfortunately, many Americans live on the outskirts of hope … some because of their poverty and some because of their color, and all too many because of both.' In order to 'help replace their despair with opportunity', Johnson continued, 'This administration today, here and now, declares unconditional war on poverty.' Johnson realized that the struggle against poverty would not be easy, but promised that 'one shall not rest until that war is won'. Poverty, Johnson declared, would be pursued 'in the city slums and small towns, in sharecropper shacks or in migrant labor camps, on Indian reservations, among whites as well as Negroes, among the young as well as the aged, in the boom towns and in the depressed areas'.

The 'War on Poverty' began when Johnson submitted the Economic Opportunity Bill to Congress in March 1964. Included among the many provisions of the Bill were plans to establish a Head Start programme for disadvantaged children of preschool age and to create a domestic version of the Peace Corps known as the Volunteers in Service to America (VISTA). To co-ordinate the 'War on Poverty' an Office of Economic Opportunity (OEO) was created. Despite some opposition from conservatives in Congress, the Economic Opportunity Bill was approved by the legislature and signed by Johnson on 20 August 1964.

Passage of the Economic Opportunity Act (1964) was a major achievement, but long before the final vote on the measure in Congress, Johnson had articulated a much broader agenda for government action. In a speech at the University of Michigan on 22 May 1964, Johnson called for the creation of a 'Great Society' in which there would be 'abundance and liberty' for all. Johnson expanded on the theme of a 'Great Society' in a speech in New York on 28 May 1964 when he declared that 'no child will go unfed and no youngster will go unschooled'. Later in the year, at a speech in Pittsburgh on 27 October 1964, Johnson further elaborated upon the 'Great Society'. 'The Great Society' he stated, 'is when America's promise and her practice come together'. More specifically, 'It's the time ... when nobody in this country is poor ... when every boy and girl in this country ... has the right to all the education that he can absorb'. Furthermore, there would be 'full social security' for 'every older man and woman' and 'a job for everyone who is willing to work, and he is going to be paid a decent wage'.

Although many of Johnson's claims about the Great Society may be dismissed as hyperbole, it is clear that his proposed agenda still went far beyond either the New Deal or the Fair Deal. Johnson was suggesting that the federal government should take action to eliminate poverty, improve education, further civil rights, ensure full employment, enhance health care and protect the environment. Such an agenda was nothing less than social engineering on a massive scale.

Johnson's vision of a Great Society was approved by the American people in the election of 1964. Running against Senator Barry Goldwater, a conservative Republican who proposed reducing rather than enlarging the role of the federal government, Johnson won a landslide victory. He won 482 electoral college votes to Goldwater's 52 electoral college votes, and polled 61 per cent of the popular vote. Democrats also did well elsewhere in the country. In both the Senate and the House of Representatives the Democrats increased their majorities. At the state level, the Democrats took twelve governorships from the Republicans, and gained over 500 more seats in the state legislatures.

Despite the size of his own victory, and the large gains made by the Democratic Party as a whole, Johnson was well aware that the mandate he had received could disappear very quickly. He therefore moved very quickly to enact the Great Society into law. At a pace unmatched since the New Deal, Johnson submitted bill after bill to Congress. In quick succession Congress enacted a bill which provided health care for the elderly and poor, and a bill which provided $1.5 billion in federal aid to elementary and secondary education. These landmark measures were followed by the Housing and Urban Development Act (1965) which appropriated $2.9 billion for urban renewal, and the Appalachian Regional Development Act (1966) which provided $1.1 billion for programmes in the depressed Appalachian region. All told, Congress enacted 435 bills in the two years following the 1964 elections. In the two years that followed, however, the pace of reform slowed as the Vietnam War began to preoccupy Johnson, and support for further legislation faded.

As the Vietnam War began to consume more and more of Johnson's time, he found it increasingly difficult to provide the leadership which was necessary for further legislative success. Without Johnson's forceful leadership, the move towards a Great Society slowed considerably as the consensus which the President had forged for his policies began to disintegrate. On the right, conservative critics began to argue that the Great Society programmes were too expensive and failed to produce the desired results. On the left, liberals began to argue about the best means of achieving the goals defined by Johnson. The result was an increase in political tension which would, on occasions, erupt into violence.

The collapse of consensus in American politics during the second half of the 1960s was to hit the civil rights movement particularly badly. With the passage of the Voting Rights Act (1965) the battle against legal segregation and political exclusion had been won. Blacks in the South found it easier to cast the vote, and could shop, eat, travel and pray in places which five years earlier had been off limits to them. As legal segregation was overcome in the South of the United States, however, the attention of the civil rights movement turned towards the plight of the black population of the cities in the North, Midwest and West of the country. Blacks in cities such as New York, Los Angeles, Detroit and Cleveland did not suffer the same legal restrictions as southern blacks. Rather, the problem confronting urban blacks was *de facto* segregation and the poverty resulting from poor employment prospects. Blacks in the cities tended to be given the lowest paid jobs. The unemployment rate among blacks was high, poverty was widespread and housing was poor. In such conditions, disillusionment with a society which proclaimed the equality of all, but then denied the black population the opportunities available to white Americans, soon turned to anger.

An indication of the growing anger of urban blacks came in the summer of 1964 when rioting broke out in Harlem, New York. The Harlem riot was the first of a series of 'ghetto rebellions' which would sweep across the United States over the next few years. In August 1965, less than a week after the signing of the Voting Rights Act (1965), blacks in the Watts district of Los Angeles took part in a week of rioting and looting which left 34 people dead, almost 4,000 rioters in prison and damage to property estimated at $40 million. Order was only restored when 12,000 national guardsmen were ordered onto the streets. In the summer of 1966 riots erupted in Chicago, Cleveland and many other cities. The following summer Newark and Detroit burst into flames. In Detroit, 43 people were killed, 7,000 arrested and $50 million worth of damage was done to property. To restore order in Detroit the federal government mobilized 15,000 national guardsmen and tanks and soldiers of the 101st Airborne Division were sent to patrol the streets. Further riots were to sweep across the United States in the summer of 1968.

The ghetto riots had a profound effect on the civil rights movement. Not only did the riots shift the geographical focus of the movement, but by raising a number of economic and social issues they also brought about a change in the style and content of black political action. Before the riots, the goal of the civil rights movement had been to secure for blacks in the South of the United States the same rights that most whites took for granted. Black demands were articulated as a call for the country to 'live out the true meaning of its creed'. The ghetto riots, however, seemed to challenge the American creed. Urban blacks were not seeking a legal accommodation with white America, but rather, were calling for a more fundamental redistribution of wealth and power. Against the background of such demands, the civil rights movement began to fragment. Unity was lost as civil rights leaders sought to confront the problems of urban blacks.

By the mid-1960s, discontent with the leadership offered by Martin Luther King led many civil rights activists to embrace the ideas articulated by Malcolm X. Malcolm had risen from a career of petty crime to become a forceful proponent of black nationalism. He preached a message of black supremacy and ridiculed non-violence as a means of promoting civil rights. 'When I was in Africa,' Malcolm declared, 'I noticed some of the Africans got their freedom faster than others .... I noticed that in the areas where independence had been gotten someone got angry. And in areas where independence had not been achieved yet, no one was angry.' In 1964 Malcolm formed the Organisation for Afro-American Unity and soon began to attract supporters from among the leadership of the civil rights movement. But shortly after the publication of his *Autobiography* in 1965, Malcolm was assassinated by gunmen from the Nation of Islam as he rose to address a black audience at the Audubon Ballroom in Harlem.

The new militancy of many within the civil rights movement became apparent in June 1966 when Willie Ricks and Stokely Carmichael began to promote the use of the slogan 'Black Power' during a civil rights march in Mississippi. Within a few weeks the slogan had spread across the country and had propelled Carmichael into a position of national prominence. But for all its appeal, 'Black Power' remained an imprecise term which was capable of being interpreted in many different ways. To some, the slogan merely expressed the growing self-belief that blacks possessed as a result of the gains made by the civil rights movement. To others, the slogan symbolized a move from the integrationist philosophy of the civil rights movement towards the black nationalism of Malcolm X. Whatever the precise meaning given to 'Black Power' by different people at different times, however, there were two important consequences of Carmichael's promotion of the slogan. First, the advocacy of 'Black Power' signalled the end of the unity of the civil rights movement. Second, the promotion of 'Black Power' caused many whites to abandon their support for the civil rights movement.

The one person to possess the authority necessary to unify the civil rights movement in the wake of the ghetto riots was Martin Luther King. On 4 April 1968, however, King was assassinated in Memphis, Tennessee, by James Earl Ray. The assassination of King effectively ended any possibility that the civil rights movement might coalesce around a new set of issues. King's death also sparked off riots in over 60 American cities. For the first time since the end of the Civil War troops were stationed outside government buildings in Washington DC to protect them from attack.

The riots in American cities have often been used as evidence that the Great Society was a failure. In many ways the expectations so forcefully articulated by the President simply foundered on the realities of life in the ghettos. Some critics have pointed out that all too often the recipients of Great Society benefits were middle-class professionals and not the poor. The expansion of housing projects, nursery education and medical care inflated both the number and the income of architects, city planners, teachers and doctors. Other critics have argued that the aims and ideals of the Great Society were undermined by the creation of a huge bureaucracy and poor administration. The poverty programme had called for local community projects with "maximum feasible participation". However, bickering, personal animosity and factionalism hampered the effectiveness of many of the projects. Daniel Moynihan believed that "maximum feasible misunderstanding" characterized the programmes more accurately.

For all the criticism levelled at the Great Society, however, millions of Americans did benefit from its programmes. Much had been achieved in the fields of civil rights, education and health care. Problems still remained, but Johnson was cheered by the fact that progress had been made. As Johnson prepared to leave office he related an anecdote he had told many times before: 'I remember a story that they told about Prime Minister Churchill toward the end of World War II days, when a little lady ... said "Mr. Prime Minister ... We are informed that if all the brandy you have drunk during this war could be poured into this room it would come up to half the room." The Prime Minister ... glumly commented, "My dear little ladies; so little have I done; so much I have yet to do."' Johnson felt the same way about the Great Society, stating 'So much do I have yet to do. But we do know that we have taken steps that had to be taken. We have marched down a road that had to be marched.'

Further reading

Vaughn Davis Burnet, *The Presidency of Lyndon B. Johnson* (Lawrence, KS, 1983).

Ronnie Dugger, *The Politician* (New York, 1982).

Henry Fairlie, *The Kennedy Promise* (Garden City, NJ, 1973).

David Garrow, *Bearing the Cross* (New York, 1986).

Herbert Parmet, *JFK* (New York, 1984).

Arthur Schlesinger, *A Thousand Days* (Boston, 1967).

9

Foreign policy in the Democratic years, 1961-1968

The transfer of power in January 1961 from the oldest elected president, Dwight Eisenhower, to the youthful John F. Kennedy, who was only 43 years old, was not simply an exercise in the surrender of age. During the election campaign Kennedy had deliberately accused the Republicans of being outdated and out of tune with contemporary change. Kennedy presented a variety of images. He cultivated an appearance of toughness and decisiveness in order to enhance his credibility as the guarantor of American power. Intellectually, he had few conventional prejudices, but he also had little of the insight that comes with long experience. He admired courage and believed in the importance of command and presence. He liked to think of himself as an intellectual, and confirmed that self-image by surrounding himself with some of the finest brains in the country.

His projection of physical courage, combined with an undoubted analytical ability, had profound and sometimes confusing consequences for his foreign policy. He projected the need for toughness in his speeches and in the presidential campaign he had waged. He had accused the Eisenhower Administration of permitting a 'missile gap' to develop. The United States, Kennedy insisted, needed to build up its nuclear arsenal to match the rate of the recent Soviet arms build-up. In the campaign he ominously accused his predecessor of offering no resistance to the establishment of Fidel Castro's communist regime on Cuba and promised to encourage and assist the resistance to the Castro regime. American power would be a force to reckon with, but only if its military hardware and will were visible and feared. At the same time he offered a revaluation of American assumptions about the international order. He said the country must 'get moving again' and in his Inaugural Address he gave clear primacy to foreign policy. He defined the goals of his administration almost exclusively in terms of the United States' international role. He set the tone of what would become the hallmark of American, and indeed western, liberalism in the 1960s: an unquestioning confidence in action, almost for its own sake.

American technolgy and know-how, he claimed, could 'abolish all forms of human poverty and all forms of human life'. He hinted at a major reassessment of the United States' responses to challenges from both the Soviet Union and the Third World. He acknowledged a world of diversity. He did recognize that not all nations would choose the liberal, capitalist path so favoured by the United States. He had a genuine sympathy for the Third World and recognized that the underdeveloped nations were more interested in agricultural yields, land reform, population control and basic literacy than they were in particular international alignments. The United States had to find a way of providing support. It could not sit on the sidelines; the Soviet Union would exploit such inaction. Kennedy issued a clarion call. The United States would pursue peace, defend human rights, aid the underdeveloped nations and oppose colonialism. But these apparently peaceful objectives would be pursued in an assertive and militant manner. Political will would overcome obstacles. What Kennedy did not make clear was what would happen if the United States' will were challenged. He knew that the United States should try and get away from the knee-jerk responses of the Dulles years. But he was also unwilling to preside over any diminution of American power.

Kennedy's first brief was the defence of the nation. He had maintained in the election campaign that the United States had lost its earlier advantage in the nuclear arms race. He also believed that the Eisenhower Administration's reliance on nuclear weapons had deprived the United States of important policy choices, and, ultimately, had reduced the level of American power. 'We intend to have a wider choice,' he declared in 1961, 'than humiliation or all-out nuclear war.' In fact his indictment of his predecessor's record was unjustified. In 1961 the United States possessed over one hundred intercontinental or intermediate ballistic missiles and eighty Polaris missiles which could be fired from submarines. It had a three to one advantage over the Soviet Union in ballistic missiles and a ten to one advantage in intercontinental bombers. Throughout his tenure as Secretatry of Defence, Robert McNamara fought a sustained battle to ensure an offensive superiority that could penetrate all conceivable Soviet defence systems. He also sought to develop a policy of 'controlled response' which aimed to limit and reduce the damage in the event of a nuclear strike. A wide range of weapons, it was argued, would give the Soviet Union an incentive for avoiding high population targets. The United States possessed sufficient Polaris and Minuteman missiles both to deter and retaliate against any Soviet first strike. An arms build-up would confirm Kennedy's resolve and would not lull the Soviet Union into thinking that his references to a diverse and complex world somehow implied a concession to changes in the balance of power.

Reliance on nuclear weapons was not enough. It would deprive policy makers of the flexibility that is necessary in a constantly changing world. The destructiveness of these weapons threatened the user as much as the adversary and thus they were irrelevant in a number of situations. In Kennedy's opinion the Eisenhower Administration had intervened in the affairs of other nations, but had been compelled to withdraw or change its plans as a result of its reliance on the ultimate weapon. The United States had to possess a military capability that could deal with conventional military encounters, particularly in Europe, or brush wars in the emerging nations. This would allow the administration to calibrate its response to particular situations more carefully and more convincingly. Incentives for limited aggression had to be reduced. According to defence strategists, if an adversary thought that the United States had only two choices, nuclear holocaust or total capitulation, and a particular dispute did not warrant risking the nuclear threat, then that adversary would be encouraged to push every opportunity. Different situations required different responses. Also a credible conventional force would serve as a graduated series of decision barriers, or 'firebreaks', between conventional and nuclear weapons. Indeed as the events of the 1960s unfolded, American leaders became increasingly convinced that the weapons of mass destruction inhibited the influence of the United States. If the United States' commitments were to be taken seriously, it had to show that it was prepared to consider the use of force. It was for these reasons that President Kennedy asked Congress for some $6 billion in new military outlays between March and July 1961.

This policy of 'flexible response' was not simply the brainchild of defence analysts. It emerged from a series of problems and crises that the new President confronted in his first months in office. By and large the President scored few foreign policy successes in the early part of his administration, at least in his relations with the Soviet Union and the communist world. The first major setback came in Cuba, where the

President authorized an American-backed attempt to overthrow Fidel Castro's regime. Throughout the latter part of the election campaign, Kennedy had made extravagant claims about eliminating the communist regime in Havana. Kennedy saw Castro as a personal challenge. His attitude at times bordered on the irrational; certainly Castro and Kennedy developed something of a vendetta against each other. But personal animosity was not the whole motivation. Cuba could be used as a Soviet military base and also as a launching-pad for revolutionary movements in other parts of Latin America. Kennedy's temptations were fed by the Cuban exiles, currently undergoing training in camps in Guatemala. These Cubans were confident that a well-planned and well-executed uprising would send Castro reeling. Above all, the President was convinced – and that was because he wanted to be convinced – during March and early April of 1961 by Allen Dulles, director of the Central Intelligence Agency, and Richard Bissell, his deputy director for operations, that the operation, which had been in the planning process for a year, would succeed. If it had succeeded it would have enhanced the President's standing enormously. Kennedy had not yet learned of bureaucratic momentum. If a man is given a task to do, he will do it and blot out the obstacles put in the way. Questions were asked; but the craving for success creates its own convenient answers. Arthur Schlesinger Jnr., one of Kennedy's earliest biographers, comments: ' The determination to keep the scheme alive sprang in part, I believe, from the embarrassments of calling it off.'

The military employment of a brigade of exiles had been conceived as an option; it was now a necessity. Caught in the whirlwind of his own ambition and his advisers' enthusiasm, Kennedy did the simplest thing: he gave the go-ahead. Logic succumbed to desire and the plan went into motion. The idea was that American-trained Cuban pilots, pretending to be defectors from the Castro regime, would knock out the Cuban air force and seize three beaches along the Cuban shore in the Zapata area around Cochinos Bay, or the Bay of Pigs, with paratroops dropping inland to control the roads. It was presumed that as news of the landings spread in Cuba, there would be a popular uprising which would swell the ranks of the rebel invaders and overthrow the Castro regime. But nothing seemed to go right. The air strikes were ineffective and not all the pilots made it back to base. On 17 April Castro's air force, still almost entirely intact, sank a ship carrying the ammunition reserve and damaged other vessels. His tanks reached the beach-heads and cut off the invasion brigade. Some never even made it to the beach as they got stuck on coral reefs. In Havana the police moved quickly, rounding up thousands of people and thus pre-empting the illusory uprising. The remaining invaders were en-circled and the enterprise disintegrated in total fiasco. One hundred and fourteen men were lost, 1,189 captured and about 150 were evacuated and made it back. Kennedy had no choice but to admit defeat and admit the responsibility was his. It was his first lesson in the limits of intervention and in his advisers' fallibility. Chester Bowles commented years later that 'the humiliating failure of the invasion shattered the myth of a New Frontier run by a breed of incisive, fault-free supermen'. In many ways it was a salutary lesson. Unfortunately, in the light of what was to happen in Vietnam, the right lessons were not immediately learned. The CIA was not trusted for a long time; and it was its warnings of the situation in Vietnam that proved to be the most accurate.

The debacle in the Bay of Pigs may have served as a signal to Premier Nikita Khrushchev of the Soviet Union to test American resolve and to reassert his own authority in the Soviet Union where several officials accused him of taking too soft a line with the West. The Soviet leader perceived a growing threat to Soviet interests. The Kennedy Administration was calling for the largest peacetime arms build-up on record and had tried to overthrow a communist gov-ernment in Cuba. In the newly-emerging nations, the People's Republic of China was competing for the role of communist protege. As early as January 1961 Khrushchev had warned that the Soviets would make a peace agreement with East Germany and thus terminate the legal basis of the western presence in West Berlin. Kennedy had no intention of surrendering to Soviet pressure. If the United States were to give up the joint occupation of the city, the structure of NATO would be undermined and guarantees of West German security would ring hollow. At their stormy summit meeting in Vienna in June 1961 the two leaders spoke of the possibility of war over the issue. 'I want peace,' Khrushchev told the President, 'but if you want war that is your problem.' Kennedy retorted that 'It will be a cold winter', and departed on that note.

The following month Kennedy appeared on national television and asked for increased defence appropriations and provisions for the calling up of reserve units. He warned that 'misjudgement on either side about the intentions of the other could rain more devastation in several hours than has been wrought in the all the wars of human history'. The following months East German troops occupied key crossing points between the eastern and western sectors and began to build the wall which divided that city until 1989. While the Wall became a depressing and shabby reminder of the divisions between East and West it served to defuse the situation by sealing off East Berlin. And it convinced the President that his tough line had averted a showdown.

The Soviets seemed intent on carrying on their war of nerves. Khrushchev took his greatest foreign policy gamble a year later, when he authorized the secret installation of nuclear missiles on the island of Cuba. By the end of August 1962, the President had received intelligence reports that an arms build-up was under-way in Cuba. Kennedy's advisers tended to see the Soviet move as an attempt by Khrushchev to test the President's resolve or to force a trade-off on American missiles in Turkey. Neither explanation is totally convincing, and reflects more on the United States' conduct of the crisis than on Khrushchev's motivation. The Soviets simply believed that the strategic balance was unfavorable to them; in many ways, the American build-up had served as a stimulus. But the Soviets' secrecy undercut any sense of legitimacy. They persuaded themselves, as powers customarily do, that the missiles were 'defensive', and not 'offensive'. In that respect the Soviet leader may have thought that the Americans would tolerate the weapons. Kennedy never hesitated in his resolve to have them removed. The issue was not the objective, which was to see the missiles removed, but how to attain it. Kennedy and his advisers were unwavering in their view that if Cuba was to become a missile base the strategic balance would have turned against the United States. Most American radar and defence systems presumed that an attack from the Soviet Union would come over the North Pole. The United States' early warning system would have been reduced from about half an hour to two minutes, hardly enough time to enact the slow firing sequence of ground-launched missiles.

In a series of secret meetings the specially constituted President's Executive Committee of the National Security Council narrowed the options to two: a surgical air strike or a blockade of the island. Kennedy's military advisers tilted towards a military showdown. Robert Kennedy, the President's brother and the principal co-ordinator of the discussions, Robert McNamara and George Ball, Undersecretary of State, wanted to provide room for manoeuvre. They advocated a blockade or 'quarantine', as it euphemistically became known, because that offered the advantage of putting the Soviet Union into the position of having to stand down or shoot first; it also gave the Americans a breathing space and the opportunity to tighten the screw, should that become necessary. On 22 October 1962 the President denounced the Soviets on television and declared the quarantine. Ships approaching Cuba would be stopped and searched; if they were found to be carrying offensive weapons they would be turned back. He ordered the armed forces to prepare for any eventuality and declared that any missile attack from Cuba against any western nation would be construed as an attack by the Soviet Union on the United States requiring a full nuclear retaliatory response.

The President retained a cool head, though many Americans feared the worst. A Gallup poll showed that one in five Americans thought World War III would break out, and three out of five thought there would be exchange of fire. Disaster was avoided. Khrushchev had no desire to go over the brink, though some of the hardliners in the Politburo wanted to call the American bluff. He ordered Soviet ships, presumably loaded with missile components, to turn back. The blockade had worked because each side wanted it to work. Kennedy offered a quid pro quo – the Americans would undertake not to invade Cuba or to try and overthrow it by force, if all existing installations were removed. The Soviets did not want a war over Cuba; as already indicated, the defence of the Castro regime was not its first priority anyway. To Castro's fury, he ordered that they be dismantled within thirty days. By 19 November all bombers and missiles had been withdrawn.

The Cuban missile crisis became something of a turning-point in East–West relations. The United States announced that it would end covert operations against Castro, though these did not come to an end for another three years. Also both leaders recognized that the existence of nuclear weapons, rather than the precise strategic balance, had averted a disaster. Thus while the Cuban missile crisis did nothing to slow down the pace of the arms race, both the Americans and the Soviets recognized that the premium on a never-ending spiral was not automatic. Rough parity in arms, or at the very least the equal ability to visit unimaginable destruction on the other, had served the two adversaries well. Above all both sides hopefully learned that crisis avoidance was better than crisis management. Since 1963 the superpowers have avoided direct showdown and have taken care to ensure, as they did during the Yom Kippur war in 1973, to orchestrate their own confrontations. Both leaders recognized that if the hawks had been permitted to prevail in either country, the outcome of the crisis might have been horribly different. In the aftermath of the crisis, levels of tension were rapidly lowered. Kennedy and McNamara developed a more modest, yet more complex, arms control strategy. New negotiations, based on the premise that the nuclear stalemate had created a common purpose between the superpowers, emerged. Agreements were to be achieved step by step. Soon a direct telephone link between the Kremlin and the White House, the 'hot line', was installed. Offending obsolete missiles were withdrawn from Turkey and, in September 1963, a Limited Test Ban Treaty, outlawing tests in the atmosphere and in space, was signed.

While Kennedy's relations with the Soviet Union consumed more headlines than any other foreign policy issue, it must not be forgotten that there were significant developments in other parts of the globe. In March 1961, with his eyes admittedly still on the Cuban revolution, Kennedy proposed an Alliance for Progress beteen the United States and Latin America. Under the scheme some $20 billion in aid was to be injected in order to modernize the semi-feudal economic structure of the continent. The President hoped to improve the image of the United States by eliminating support for dictatorial regimes, based on feudal land tenure and the flight of capital. In Africa, despite continued investment in white southern Africa, the President welcomed the stream of decolonization and actively solicited the company of the leaders of the new nations. The distinctive spirit of the New Frontier was reflected in the Peace Corps, which had been inspired by Roosevelt's Civilian Conservation Corps of 1933. Established initially by executive order in March 1961, the Peace Corps hoped to mobilize the idealism of the young. College-age volunteers would be sent to underdeveloped countries, where they would assist in irrigation projects, the teaching of basic literacy, birth control drives and other social programmes. The Peace Corps harnessed the idealism of the young to the crusade against communism to show that western liberalism had more to offer the Third World than its communist competitor. While Kennedy and his advisers undoubtedly had a greater appreciation of the obstacles faced by the underdeveloped nations, they still believed that American interests could only be protected by the spread of liberal ideology. Kennedy's ambition to land a man on the moon had as much to do with international competion as it did with scientific challenge. 'If we can get to the moon before the Soviets, we should' he told journalists.

This ambitious liberalism would meet its hubris in the Far East. The United States leadership was still convinced that the communist world was monolithic. It failed to recognize that the People's Republic of China under Mao Zedong had embarked on a rather different course of industrial and agricultural development and that it competed with, rather than complemented, the Soviet Union for the economic and ideological leadership of revolutionary movements in the Third World. In addition, while the United States had paid lip service to the process of decolonization it had failed to understand the forces that had been unleashed by the dismantling of the European empires. The President's advisers had become rather self-assured as a result of the successful execution of the Cuban missile crisis. It had bred a confidence in the ability to score similar successes in other settings. Graduated escalating pressures might work in a superpower context, but they would not necessarily work in a developing country with rather different concerns and political disciplines. However, the United States had to learn this slowly and painfully in Vietnam.

The United States' involvement was not a sudden development. After the Second World War it had provided assistance to the French in their attempt to hold on to their empire in Indochina and had seriously considered direct military involvement in 1954. After the French had been defeated Indochina was divided into separate states, and Vietnam itself became a divided nation after the communists fled to the northern half and anti-communists to the southern. When countrywide elections failed to materialize, the division became a consolidation and, in effect, two separate states emerged. The United States became deeply committed to the regime in the South. The new regime there was totally dependent on American aid to sustain it in its resistance to the growing threat of destabilization from communists, who began to filter south in large numbers after 1959. By the time Eisenhower left office, nearly 80 per cent of the aid received by South Vietnam went on military assistance; it was already the fifth largest recipient of American aid. Thus Kennedy inherited a substantial commitment, though it must be emphasized it was not an inextricable one.

However, Kennedy's foreign policy style made such extrication more difficult. Despite repeated references to the fate of the Vietnamese people, the Kennedy Administration was more concerned about its own position and image in the world. Indeed, the Americans did not even identify the enemy consistently. The enemy's location seemed to shift from Moscow to Beijing to Hanoi and even to dissidents at home. But that lay in the future. At the beginning of the Kennedy Administration the conflict in Vietnam between North and South, between South Vietnamese communists (Vietcong) and the Diem government, and between rival religious factions in the South, was not at the centre of foreign policy concerns; the administration's evaluation of the situation in Vietnam was determined by events elsewhere and by the United States conduct of its rivalry with the Soviet Union. There were two overriding concerns. The first was the dangerous superpower competition; Kennedy and his advisers were convinced that the problems in Indochina could not be disentangled from that rivalry. If the communists succeeded in toppling the American-backed regime of Ngo Dinh Diem, it would enhance Soviet power. The second driving force for involvement in Vietnam lay in the public philosophy of liberalism in the 1960s. Many planners believed that social and political reconstruction was a legitimate and challenging brief for government. If the United States wished to establish the credibility of its liberal credentials throughout the world, it had to demonstrate its efficacy. The system had to be seen to work. The confident enthusiasm of the New Frontiersmen propelled them into a vortex that would come to tear that confidence asunder. To them, Vietnam seemed a good test case. The position of President Ngo Dinh Diem was deteriorating rapidly. The United States had the opportunity to confront the Soviet Union, to prove its fidelity to its commitments, to demonstrate the effectiveness of the flexible response strategy and to create a laboratory for American liberal government. Various emissaries and missions were sent to South Vietnam to analyse and report on developments. Practically all of them sent back reports which were optimistic about the prospects of stabilizing South Vietnam. Largely as a result of gradual but isolated decisions, the number of military advisers in Vietnam grew from about 2,000 when Kennedy took office to over 16,000 by the time of his assassination.

The President believed that Vietnam was a good proving ground. He never was forced to make a single, crucial decision on the worsening conflict in Vietnam that would require the kind of intense pondering that the missile crisis had occasioned. The fateful steps were taken by Lyndon Baines Johnson, who succeeded Kennedy after his assassination in Dallas on 22 November 1963. In many ways Johnson fell victim to his own earlier political success and the sense of determination that enshrouded liberals as a result of Kennedy's murder. Johnson wanted policies that would succeed. He was happy to assume the civil rights slogan of 'we shall overcome'. Despite his formidable experience in domestic politics, he was unfamiliar with foreign affairs. Foreign affairs represented an uncertain world that was not readily malleable to the kinds of pressures that could be applied in Congress or the State house. No problem was insoluble. To Johnson the Vietnam problem was a problem between people with different but negotiable interests. He could not grasp that the war in Vietnam was a massive ideological struggle, one that was not susceptible to compromise. Civil wars are almost never resolved by negotiation and compromise. He needed to believe that a combination of resolve and high purpose would sway the National Liberation Front and his supporters at home. His Vietnamese opponents were not interested and his constituency at home slowly evaporated as the facts on the ground gave the lie to the claims from the White House. Because Johnson's claims were often extravagant he was often accused of deceit; in fact, he deceived nobody more than himself.

Johnson, like Kennedy, believed that the the defence of South-East Asia was crucial to the maintenance of world order. If the United States did not defend it, it would lose credibility with both allies and rivals. The problem was that this notion of 'credibility' created a self-imposed straitjacket. The continued defence of Vietnam became logically necessary. Johnson never intended to wage a full-scale war; indeed, he invariably gave his generals less in the way of material support than they wanted. The war was carefully calibrated, in accordance with the principles of flexible response. Johnson constantly calculated that the United States could force all parties in the dispute to the conference table by meeting each new application of force with an even more forceful response. The real escalation began in August 1964 when two American destroyers were attacked in the Tonkin Gulf by Norh Vietnamese gunboats. Johnson disregarded the issue of American provocation and secured the passage of a Senate resolution which gave the President almost limitless power to counter the attack with armed force. The South Vietnamese government seemed to be in a state of collapse. Between the death of Diem in November 1963 and the rise of the more stable regime of President Nguyen Thieu and Marshal Nguyen Cao Ky there had been nine changes of government. So when in February 1965 the Vietcong attacked two American air bases at Pleiku and Quinhon, killing thirty-one Americans, Johnson saw his opportunity to establish that credibility. He ordered the systematic and sustained aerial bombing of North Vietnam. In March he deployed 3,500 marines to Da Nang; by the summer there were 50,000 men in Vietnam. At the end of the year there were 184,000 men; by the end of 1966 there were 385,000 and 486,000 by the end of 1967. At the height of the war there were about 550,000 men serving in Vietnam.

This rapid and largely unforeseen escalation had effects that were the opposite of those intended. Johnson and his advisers presumed that the North Vietnamese, the Vietcong and their suppliers in China and the Soviet Union would understand the extent of the American determination and taper off their infiltration of the South and agree to a negotiated settlement. Johnson also hoped that such rapid rein-forcements would bolster the sagging morale of the Saigon govern-ment. But because each escalation was carefully matched as a response to the communists' military offensives, Johnson in effect relinquished the initiative to the other side. Johnson's claim that he was acting to preserve the balance of power was unconvincing. It was also never quite clear who, precisely, was being deterred by the United States' military involvement. The Chinese were identified as the principal suppliers of the North Vietnamese but the United States was always careful not to provoke a direct Chinese intervention. Above all, the South Vietnamese seemed to suffer more from the American air attacks than did their foes in the North. Double the tonnage of bombs was dropped on the South than on the North. The United States' military strategy also helped the enemy. Defoliants were used in its bombing campaigns to clear the countryside of guerillas. This alien-ated the very people the Americans were purporting to defend and forced a sizeable proportion of South Vietnam's rural population into the towns. The growing refugee problem created social unrest and generated more dissidence. Above all, forced urbanization and popu-lation concentration made a military defeat easier when the final assault came in 1975. Guerilla operations in the cities, and in particular the one launched in February 1968, the Tet offensive, when commu-nist forces succeeded in penetrating the cities, including Saigon, had paradoxically been made possible by the United States' bombing strategy.

The surprise Vietcong offensive during the Buddhist festival of Tet unleashed a storm of criticism and an agonizing reappraisal of Ameri-can policy on the home front as well. Although the offensive ended with a tactical defeat and very high losses for the Vietcong, the intractability of the war was made clear and dramatized by the lurid and shocking newsreels that appeared almost nightly on television. Americans were appalled by moving images of young girls writhing in agony as napalm burned on their backs or by the spectre of a young Vietcong captive having his brains summarily blown out in broad daylight in the streets of Saigon. Pacifists and men and women who had opposed the war on ideological grounds, so-called 'doves', were joined by large numbers of Americans who believed quite simply that the United States could not win the war by continuing with its destructive and restrictive military strategy, and they were unwilling to contemplate a further intensification. If the cause had been once worthwhile, it was no longer so. The physical and political damage outweighed whatever benefits had been thought to exist. It was no longer worth the effort. Senator Eugene McCarthy of Minnesota ran in the March Democratic primary in New Hampshire on a peace platform and won 40 per cent of the vote. Johnson saw the writing on the wall and announced that he would not seek another nomination. Some vocal opponents of the war, many of them middle-class students whose parents had been active supporters of Democratic liberalism, not only took to the streets to demonstrate against the war but also began to question and even reject the entire ethos on which they had been brought up. The alienation produced by the war in Vietnam reverberated in other areas. The young, many of them highly educated, began to use drugs quite openly and to flaunt their sexuality even more. They turned their backs on employment in government, commerce or industry to join communes or just 'drop out'. In the universities, students rejected curricula that had served for decades and instead they demanded 'relevant' courses in black or women's studies and formal participation in the decision-making process of the universities. Blacks, particularly in the cities, joined militant organizations and rejected Christianity altogether. While disaffection with the Vietnam war was not the single cause of these phenomena, it was usually cited as the most outstanding example of the inhuman consequences of postwar liberalism. In short, dissidents saw the Vietnam war as the logical consequence of the liberal malaise.

The peace candidacies of Eugene McCarthy and Robert Kennedy, who was shot dead in June 1968 by a deranged Palestinian, and the very serious demonstrations and civil disturbances that occurred during the 1968 Democratic convention in Chicago, pointed to the deleterious effect the war in South-East Asia was having on the home front. Wars are traditionally thought to unite nations. This war divided the United States as no recent war had done. Both major candidates, Hubert Humphrey for the Democrats, and Richard Nixon, standing for the Republican party, pledged that they would wind down the war. Nixon won the election in November and began the long process of ending American involvement. As things turned out the war lasted longer and inflicted more damage under President Nixon than under Lyndon Johnson. But the motor for the United States' eventual withdrawal had begun in 1968. The war in Vietnam also became a turning-point in the United States' foreign policy as the architects of that policy recognized that American military power and economic resources were limited. Johnson had already begun to open avenues with the Soviet Union, but the very logic of the Vietnam war prevented any real exploration of the alternatives to confrontation. The war had not only eroded the domestic consensus for his Great Society programme, it had also constricted the possibilities of reexamining the international order. The war had been fought primarily to establish the United States' 'credibility'. It served only to prevent the development of an early rapprochement with the communist and Third Worlds and actually caused divisions or at least resentments within the western alliance. By 1968 the United States would have been hard-pressed anywhere else in the world if a comparable military crisis had emerged. Its intellectual resources were also stretched. The strains in the NATO alliance resulting from French intransigence, the Arab–Israeli war of June 1967 and the Soviet invasion of Czechoslovakia in 1968 were treated with little regard to their wider contexts. The financial costs of the Vietnam war were astronomic. According to McNamara's own estimates, for the fiscal year 1966 the war was adding $9.4 billion to the normal peacetime defence expenditure and $19.7 billion for 1967. For the time being at least the United States would have to look long and hard at its capabilities and its commitments overseas. The experience in Vietnam would cast its shadow over future policy-makers for a long time to come. But nothing lasts forever.

Further reading

John L. Gaddis, *Strategies of Containment: A Critical Appraisal of Postwar National Security Policy* (New York, 1982).

David Halberstam, *The Best and the Brightest* (New York, 1972).

George C. Herring, *America's Longest War: The United States and Vietnam, 1950-1975* (New York, 1979).

Herbert S. Parmet, *JFK: The Presidency of John F. Kennedy* (London, 1984).

Thomas G. Paterson (ed.), *Kennedy's Quest for Victory: American Foreign Policy 1961-1963* (New York, 1989).

Herbert Y. Schandler, *The Unmaking of a President: Lyndon Johnson and Vietnam* (Princeton, 1977).

10

Years of stagflation, 1968-1980

The twelve years from 1968 to 1980 were a traumatic period for the United States. Domestically, rising crime, a sense of permissiveness, political assassination, inflation, unemployment and political scandal combined to undermine confidence in the federal government. Overseas, the problem posed by Vietnam, and the perception of growing Soviet power seemed to call into question the United States' position in the world. In short, the political order which had been created by the crises of the Great Depression and the Second World War appeared to be on the verge of breaking down. Increasingly, the political truths of an entire generation appeared to be cast into doubt as the country seemed to flounder. It was a period when, for most Americans, uncertainty and confusion replaced confidence and clarity.

Underlying the political crisis of the late 1960s was an economic malaise which cast into question the federal government's ability to satisfy the rising expectations of the American people. Although the New Deal political order had been born in the midst of a Depression, the interest group state it had spawned had been sustained by economic growth. It was economic growth which allowed the federal government to provide help and resources to disadvantaged groups, and it was economic strength which enabled the United States to project its power across the world. By the late 1960s, however, it was clear that the American economy was in trouble. Whereas the United States had led the world in economic growth during the first two decades of the post-war period, by 1967 the country's economic pre-eminence had been reduced. Over the next decade or so the United States' relative economic decline would become only too apparent. Between 1967 and 1975 Japan, Germany, France, Italy, and Britain all had greater rates of growth in manufacturing output than the United States.

The roots of the relative economic decline of the United States can be traced, in part, to the economic recovery of the European nations and Japan after the Second World War. In certain respects the degree of the United States' economic pre-eminence during the first two decades of the postwar period was a consequence of the Second World War, and a decline in that pre-eminence was only to be expected as the other countries slowly rebuilt their industries. Like many other countries the United States also suffered when the Organisation of Petroleum Exporting Countries (OPEC) quadrupled the price of oil in December 1973, largely in response to American support for Israel in the Yom Kippur War. Changes in the international economic climate alone, however, do not fully explain this relative economic decline. The roots of decline also lie in the very nature of the political order created by Roosevelt and nurtured by his successors, and in the United States' very emergence as a superpower. Quite simply, the country did not have the resources to meet its commitments, both domestic and foreign. It could not bear the cost of fighting a War on Poverty and the Vietnam War. Like many great powers before it, the United States had overextended itself.

The fact that the United States had commitments which were far in excess of its resources contributed to the country's relative economic decline in two ways. First, in an attempt to satisfy domestic and foreign expectations the country was forced to use resources which could otherwise have been used for capital investment. By 1975, for example, the United States had a lower rate of investment than any of its major competitors: a fact which helps explain why American industry became uncompetitive during this period. Markets were lost and unemployment rose as a consequence. Second, during the 1960s, the Vietnam War and the Great Society programmes were financed without raising taxation. Over time such a policy merely contributed to the inflationary pressures that were being generated by an expanding world economy. In short, the two economic evils of the 1970s - high inflation and high unemployment - had domestic as well as overseas origins. The stagflating economy was as much a consequence of the New Deal political system and the United States' emergence as a superpower, as it was a consequence of uncontrollable events elsewhere in the world.

One effect of the poor performance of the American economy during this period was to force a change in the political agenda. Instead of determining domestic and overseas priorities within the context of an expanding economy, Presidents Richard Nixon, Gerald Ford and Jimmy Carter faced the much more difficult problem of managing the United States' relative decline. The expectations of domestic groups needed to be lowered and overseas commitments reassessed. To do this meant challenging the public philosophy of a generation and reconsidering what were believed to be the immutable truths of the country's geopolitical situation. In short, the reality of economic decline forced Presidents Nixon, Ford and Carter to challenge the prevailing orthodoxies of the New Deal and the Cold War.

The election of 1968 in fact presented the voters with a clear choice between two candidates who offered distinct answers to the country's problems. In March 1968 President Johnson surprised the nation by declaring at the end of a television address on Vietnam that: 'I shall not seek and I will not accept the nomination of my party for another term as your President.' Many observers have argued that Johnson's decision not to seek another term in office was a result of his feeling that the voters were dissatisfied with his policies in Vietnam. Others have suggested that the cause was to be found in his failure to end racial unrest in the cities. Whatever the reasons for Johnson's withdrawal from the race, however, his decision, together with the assassination of Senator Robert F. Kennedy in June 1968, left the way clear for the Vice-President Hubert H. Humphrey to secure the Democratic nomination. Closely identified with both the domestic, and foreign, policies of the Johnson Administration, Humphrey campaigned to continue the war in Vietnam and pursue the objectives of the Great Society. This view of the future was challenged in 1968 by both the Republican candidate, Richard M. Nixon, and George C. Wallace, a former Governor of Alabama, who was running as an independent. While Nixon sought to appeal to 'Middle America' by championing the cause of a middle-class disillusioned with the politics of the Great Society and promised 'peace with honor' in Vietnam, Wallace sought to take advantage of the fears of those concerned with the spread of urban riots, the growth of the welfare state and the rise of the federal government, and argued that the only satisfactory solution to the war in Vietnam was a total American victory.

Although there was never any possibility that George Wallace would win the election, the result was close enough to support the supposition that his campaign had an impact on the final outcome. Nixon defeated Humphrey by approximately 500,000 votes, a margin of one percentage point. In terms of electoral college votes, however, Nixon's victory was more decisive. He received 302 electoral college votes compared with Humphrey's 191. In the best showing by a third party candidate since 1924, Wallace won 10 million popular votes, 13.5 per cent of the total, and 46 electoral college votes. Perhaps of more importance, though, was the geographical distribution of votes. Nixon won all but four of the states which were west of the Mississippi, while Humphrey's support was concentrated in the Northeast. Many pundits argued that such a distribution signalled the end of the New Deal Democratic coalition and the emergence of a Republican majority, at least at the presidential level. If the southern states which had voted for Wallace could be brought into the Republican fold then future Republican victories would be assured.

In an attempt to entice white southerners away from the Democratic Party and into the Republican Party President Nixon launched what became known as his 'southern strategy'. This involved a concerted effort to reduce the federal government's involvement in promoting civil rights. In 1970, for example, Nixon sought to prevent the US Congress from renewing the Voting Rights Act of 1965. He also tried to delay the implementation of court orders requiring the desegregation of school districts in Mississippi, and end the practice of busing students to obtain racially mixed schools. Busing had aroused passions. Its supporters firmly believed that whatever disruption it caused, it was a crucial step towards bringing the races together. Its opponents argued that disturbing children's access to neighbourhood school and social networks was too dear in an experiment which was uncertain anyway. In all three areas, however, Nixon was unsuccessful. Not only did Congress extend the Voting Rights Act over Nixon's veto, but the Supreme Court in *Alexander v. Holmes County Board of Education* (1969) ordered a quick end to segregation, and then in *Swann v. Charlotte-Mecklenburg Board of Education* (1971) ruled that cities must bus students out of their neighbourhoods if this was necessary to achieve integration. Nixon then asked Congress to impose a moratorium on all busing orders by the Supreme Court. The House of Representatives complied with Nixon's wishes, but the antibusing bill was defeated in the US Senate. Opponents of busing finally won a small victory in 1974 when the Supreme Court ruled in *Milliken v. Bradley* that desegregation plans in Detroit which required students to be bused from the inner city to the suburbs were unconstitutional.

Milliken v. Bradley (1974) marked a shift away from the unambiguous liberalism of the Warren Court. Nixon was fortunate in being able to make four appointments to the Court. Warren Burger, his first appointment, was not controversial. Nixon's next two nominations, however, encountered considerable oppposition in the Senate. Clement F. Haynsworth, a federal appeals court judge from South Carolina, was rejected by the Senate when it became known that he had heard a case involving a corporation in which he held stock. The nomination of Harold Causwell, an appeals court judge from Florida, was even more controversial. Causwell had a record of opposing civil rights for blacks, and was generally regarded as lacking in ability. When the Senate rejected Causwell, Nixon took care to nominate jurists of stature to the Court. The subsequent nominations of Harry Blackmun, Lewis Powell and William Rehnquist encountered little opposition.

Although motivated by the desire to achieve the political end of attracting white southerners into the Republican Party, President Nixon's 'southern strategy' was consistent with the general aims of his domestic policy. At the centre of Nixon's approach to domestic affairs was a belief that the federal government had grown too large and needed trimming. To achieve this end Nixon moved on two broad fronts. First, he submitted proposals to Congress which would have reduced the size of the federal bureaucracy. Typical of this approach was the Family Assistance Plan (FAP) which Nixon submitted to Congress in 1969. This proposal aimed to overhaul the welfare system and streamline the bureaucracy created by the Great Society programmes. Rather than receive a range of different benefits, the FAP proposed paying poor families a direct grant of $1,600. In other words, it would guarantee them an income. The FAP, however, was defeated in Congress. Second, Nixon sought to reduce the influence of the federal government by restoring the state governments as centres of policy-making. Calling his programme the 'New Federalism', Nixon gained the approval of Congress for a 'revenue-sharing plan' in 1972, which consolidated $30 billion of federal grants earmarked for specific projects within individual states into block grants, which the state governments could then spend according to their own priorities.

Despite Congress's acceptance of the 'revenue-sharing plan', the 'New Federalism' failed to change the relationship between the federal government and the state governments which had developed in the forty years since the New Deal. Understanding why this should be the case is not particularly difficult. Quite simply, too many people had a vested interest in the existing system. Members of Congress, Governors, State Legislators, interest groups and individuals all benefited in one way or other from federal grants for specific projects: the politicians because they could refer at election time to the work they had done to bring the resources into the state; the groups and individuals because they were the recipients of those resources. Breaking such a network of interests was simply beyond the power of President Nixon, particularly as he was the first new President since 1849 to confront a Congress in which both chambers were under the control of the opposition party. Indeed, at the same time that Nixon was talking about reducing the size of the federal government Congress was busy enacting legislation which added to the bureaucracy's pervasiveness. Typical were the Mine Safety and Health Act (1969), the Occupational Safety and Health Act (1970) and the Consumer Product Safety Act (1972). Together with measures which indexed the level of social security benefits to the rate of inflation, and increased the level of food stamp funding, the net result of Congress's activism was a more rapid rise in spending on social programmes than had been achieved even during the Great Society.

In addition to legislation which increased spending on social programmes, Congress also responded to growing popular pressure to protect the environment. Evidence that many of man's activities were damaging the environment had long been available. In 1962 Rachel Carson's book *Silent Spring* had painted a devastating picture of the effects of pesticides on the animal and plant life of the United States. It was not until the late 1960s, however, that Congress took concerted action to address environmental concerns. Among the most important of the environmental laws passed during this period were the Clean Air Act (1970) and the National Environmental Policy Act (1970). Concern for the environment was soon to fade, though, as the economy declined. Many industrialists complained that the United States' environmental laws were imposing a cost on them which their competitors did not have to suffer. Few Americans were willing to suffer a cut in their standard of living to protect the environment.

Although President Nixon's domestic record was uninspiring, the perceived success of his foreign policy, together with the Democrats' choice of the liberal Senator George McGovern of South Dakota as their presidential candidate, virtually ensured the President's re-election in 1972. The only threat to Nixon came from George Wallace, who as a third-party candidate had the potential to attract conservative votes away from the Republicans. This threat was removed, however, when Wallace was forced to withdraw from the campaign after being shot and left paralysed on 15 May 1972. Wallace's withdrawal left the way clear for Nixon to win a landslide victory. Nixon received 47,169,000 popular votes to McGovern's 29,170,000. He won every state except Massachusetts and the District of Columbia, receiving 520 electoral college votes to McGovern's 17. It was the greatest electoral triumph ever achieved by a Republican presidential candidate.

Nixon, however, was not able to enjoy his triumph for very long. During the election campaign, Senator McGovern had often complained about the 'dirty tricks' of the Nixon Administration, but his complaints had generally been viewed as the protestations of a losing candidate. Thus when five men were arrested inside the Democratic National Headquarters, which was situated in the Watergate complex in Washington DC, the story attracted very little attention. It was only after the election that the full story of the Nixon Administration's involvement in the Watergate affair became apparent. Under questioning by Judge John J. Sirica, one of the men arrested began to detail his connections with the White House. James W. McCord, a security chief for the Nixon campaign organisation – the Committee to Re-elect the President (CREEP) – revealed that there had been an attempted cover-up of the break-in by persons at the highest levels of the Nixon Administration. Over the next two years further investigations revealed a web of intrigue which would end in the first resignation of an American President, and the conviction and imprisonment of twenty-five of his officials, including four cabinet members.

The line of investigation pursued first by Judge Sirica, then Special Prosecutor Archibald Cox and then the Senate Select Committee on Presidential Campaign Activities under the chairmanship of the Democratic Senator Sam J. Ervin of North Carolina, led directly to the White House. Among the most important witnesses who appeared before the Ervin Committee were White House Chief of Staff H.R. Haldeman, White House domestic advisor John Erlichman, special counsel to the President John Dean and former Attorney-General John N. Mitchell. Dean testified that Mitchell, with the knowledge of Haldeman and Erlichman, had authorized the Watergate break-in, and that Nixon had approved the cover-up. These accusations were denied by Mitchell, Haldeman and Erlichman who testified that Nixon had no foreknowledge of either the break-in or the cover-up. When it emerged during the testimony given to the Ervin Committee that Nixon's conversations in the White House had been taped since the beginning of 1971, Special Prosecutor Cox made a strenuous effort to obtain the tapes pertaining to Watergate in an effort to uncover the extent of the President's involvement in the affair. Nixon refused to comply with Cox's request, however, and in a rather self-defeating action ordered Cox to be dismissed. Not only did Attorney-General Elliot Richardson and Deputy Attorney-General William Ruckelshaus prefer to resign rather than execute the order, but Congress began impeachment proceedings against Nixon. Moreover, Cox's replacement as Special Prosecutor, Leon Jaworski, proved to be no more pliable than his predecessor. Jaworski continued to make efforts to obtain the tapes, and on 24 July 1974 the Supreme Court finally ruled in the case *U.S. v. Nixon* that the President had to surrender the tapes.

A few days after the Supreme Court's ruling, the House Judiciary Committee voted to recommend three articles of impeachment against Nixon. The first article accused him of obstructing justice through the withholding of evidence. The second article charged him with abusing power by using federal agencies like the FBI to deprive citizens of their constitutional rights. The third article accused him of unconstitutionally defying the subpoenas of the House Judiciary Committee. Before the House of Representatives as a whole could vote on the articles of impeachment, however, Nixon decided to resign. On 9 August 1974 he formally proffered his letter of resignation to Secretary of State Henry Kissinger, and was succeeded as President by Vice-President Gerald Ford. One month after assuming office Ford issued a pardon to Nixon for any crime that he might have committed while occupying the presidential office.

Richard Nixon was the first President in history of the United States to resign, and was generally castigated for bringing the office into disrepute. On a more general level, his activities served to erode public confidence in the institutions of American government. One opinion poll taken in 1974 revealed that only 14 per cent of those questioned had any faith in the executive branch of government. Perhaps the most important task faced by President Ford, therefore, was to restore the public's confidence in the presidency. His early attempts to 'cleanse the air', however, were soon overshadowed by his pardon of Nixon. Although there is no evidence to suggest that Nixon and Ford had concluded a deal, the result of the pardon was to taint Ford with Watergate. Thus, far from killing the issue once and for all, Ford's action served only to prolong the scandal, and alienate the

Democratic-controlled Congress. Within a month of assuming office Ford had managed to erode the natural sympathy that many members of Congress had originally felt towards him. Thereafter, relations between the two institutions of government were to be characterized by conflict. In his fifteen months as President Ford vetoed 39 bills, far outstripping the previous record which had been set by Herbert Hoover.

The main focus of the conflict between President Ford and the US Congress was the state of the economy. By 1974 the United States was suffering from both high inflation and a high rate of unemployment; a development which seemed to undermine traditional Keynesian techniques of controlling the economy through the management of demand. With opinion divided as to the best approach to dealing with the stagflating economy, President Ford decided to concentrate his efforts on curbing inflation. To this end he advocated such measures as a sharp reduction in government spending, higher taxes and the levying of higher duties on imported petroleum. Most members of Congress, on the other hand, advocated tax cuts and an increase in government spending as a means of reflating the economy. As the rates of inflation and unemployment continued to worsen in 1975, however, Ford was forced to change his priorities. Concluding that unemployment was just as bad as inflation he recommended an anti-recession programme to Congress which included both a tax cut of $16 billion for people with an annual income of less that $40,000, and a plan for public-service employment. Unfortunately, unemployment and inflation continued to rise. At the end of 1976 the inflation rate was 9 per cent while the unemployment rate stood at just over 8 per cent.

With the economy performing so poorly, Gerald Ford came close to being rejected by his party for the Republican nomination in 1976. He was only just able to beat off a strong challenge by Ronald Reagan, a former Governor of California, who appealed to the right wing of the party. After gaining the Republican nomination, however, Ford came surprisingly close to defeating his Democratic opponent Jimmy Carter, a former Governor of Georgia. Carter had enjoyed an enormous lead in the early opinion polls, but by the day of the election his lead had practically disappeared. In the event, though, Ford was not quite able to overcome Carter's early advantage. Carter received 40,180,000 popular votes to Ford's 38,435,000, and won 297 electoral college votes to Ford's 241.

Carter triumphed at the polls because he was able to capitalize on the cynicism that many Americans felt towards the federal government in the wake of Watergate. Early in his campaign, Carter had promised that 'I will never tell a lie to the American people', and during a televised debate with President Ford had told the viewers that 'Anything you don't like about Washington, I suggest you blame on him.' In short, Carter had won the election by running against the government in Washington DC. Like Eisenhower before him, he was an outsider called upon to restore faith in government.

At the beginning of his presidency, Carter took several steps to bring a 'common touch' to the office. After his inauguration he walked down Pennsylvania Avenue instead of riding in a limousine. He also dressed informally when giving televised 'fire side' chats. Such gimmicks, however, could not disguise the almost insurmountable problems that Carter faced. Like Nixon and Ford before him, he was expected to revive the economy and reassert the United States' power around the world, and just like his two predecessors, it was a task at which he was doomed to fail.

Although the rhetoric of the election campaign suggested that there would be pronounced differences between the Ford and Carter Administrations, in practice there was little change. Carter's promises of full employment, national health care, welfare reform, tax reform, aid to the cities, a new energy policy and government reorganization were largely left on the campaign trail as the full implications of the nation's economic problems became apparent to the new President. The aims of his domestic programmes became secondary to the need to restore the economic strength of the United States, while the direction of his foreign policy was thrown into disarray by the unforeseen actions of other nations like Iran. That Carter's efforts should ultimately end in failure should come as no surprise though. Not only did the enormous difference between what the American people expected a President to be able to achieve, and what in fact he had the power to achieve, make failure almost inevitable, but Carter's commitments to balance the budget and curb inflation imposed severe constraints on his ability to achieve his other goals.

In contrast to his predecessor, President Carter determined at the beginning of his Administration to tackle the unemployment component of stagflation rather than the inflation component. His methods of dealing with the problem, however, were exactly the same as those used by Nixon and Ford: tax cuts and increased public spending. In

1977 an economic stimulative package was passed by Congress which included $15 billion in tax cuts and $15 billion in job creation schemes. As a result of these measures, the unemployment rate declined from 8 per cent to 7 per cent in 1977. By 1978 unemployment was down to 5.7 per cent, its lowest level since 1974. The rate of inflation, however, began to spiral out of control, reaching 10 per cent in 1978. Fearing the consequences of an accelerating inflation rate, Carter abandoned his programme for dealing with unemployment, and instead turned his attention to this other spectre of stagflation. In doing so he reversed his earlier policies. He tried to delay the implementation of the tax reductions and public spending programmes which he had proposed in his first year. Far from curing inflation, this helter skelter approach to economic management merely contributed to the problem of the stagflating economy. By 1980, the unemployment rate stood at 7.5 per cent, the inflation rate at just over 12 per cent, and interest rates at an historical high of 20 per cent.

The problems facing President Carter were compounded in 1979 when an upsurge of violence in the Middle East produced a fuel shortage in the United States. Motorists were forced to queue for petrol, the price of oil rose and Carter's standing in opinion polls dropped to an all-time low. In the summer of 1979, an opinion poll showed Carter with an approval rating of 26 per cent, far lower than even President Nixon had suffered at the height of the Watergate crisis. Chastened by the opinion polls, Carter spent ten days at Camp David with his closest advisers trying to find a solution to the country's problems. When Carter emerged from his retreat, however, he could only talk about a 'crisis of confidence' and a need for 'a rebirth of the American spirit'. Few people were reassured by such generalities.

For all of President Carter's efforts to provide a sense of direction, by 1980 most Americans believed that their country was drifting without a sense of purpose. Its economy was in a shambles, and a number of foreign policy reverses suggested that the country had lost its ability to impose its will upon the world. The public philosophy which had prevailed in the country since the New Deal appeared to be discredited, leaving a vacuum in public life. All in all, the way was clear for a new President who could offer the country a new sense of direction, could restore its faith in itself and proffer solutions to its many problems.

Further reading

Stephen Ambrose, *Nixon*, 2 vols. (New York, 1987, 1989).

Hal Bochin, *Richard Nixon* (New York, 1980).

Michael A. Genovese, *The Nixon Presidency* (New York, 1990).

Betty Glad, *Jimmy Carter* (New York, 1980).

Edwin C. Hargrove, *Jimmy Carter As President* (Baton Rouge, 1988).

Haynes Johnson, *In The Absence of Power* (New York, 1980).

Lawrence H. Shoup, *The Carter Presidency and Beyond* (Palo Alto, CA, 1980).

Theodore H. White, *Breach of Faith* (New York, 1975).

Robert Woodward and Carl Bernstein, *All The President's Men* (New York, 1974).

11

From detente to national malaise, 1969-1980

When Richard Nixon entered the White House in January 1969 he was confronted with the task of reassessing many of the basic tenets which had guided American foreign policy since the end of the Second World War. Although the Vietnam War, with its stark message of the limits of American power, acted as a catalyst for change, the need for a fundamental reassessment of policy lay in much broader changes in the world. In 1945 the United States dominated the world in a way that few countries, if any, had achieved before. Not only did the United States enjoy economic dominance over a world shattered by war, but the country's possession of the atomic bomb gave it unparalleled military power. By 1968 the limits of American military and economic power were clear for all to see. The armies of the United States were being humbled in the jungles of South-East Asia, its monopoly of atomic weapons had long disappeared, and its economic prominence was being challenged by Japan and West Germany. In short, the world had changed in the years since 1945, and old policies had little worth in a new world.

Unlike his two immediate predecessors, Nixon possessed some foreign policy experience and was willing to devote a considerable portion of his time to dealings with other nations. In formulating policy Nixon was assisted by Henry Kissinger. Kissinger was to dominate foreign affairs for almost a decade. A former professor at Harvard University, Kissinger served first as National Security Adviser to Nixon, and then as Secretary of State under both Nixon and Ford. Like former Secretaries of State John Foster Dulles, Dean Acheson and Dean Rusk, he believed the United States to be in a worldwide struggle for supremacy with the Soviet Union and China. Unlike them, however, Kissinger believed that a worldwide permanent peace was achievable. A world order, based on the balance of power, would have to be negotiated and managed by the superpowers. In essence, he viewed foreign policy as a game of chess. Small countries were pawns to be moved around the board with the concurrence of the world's political leaders, in order to achieve the desired outcome.

The first step in Henry Kissinger's master plan was to engineer an end to the Vietnam War. Kissinger believed that the war in Vietnam distracted the United States' attention away from more important interests in Europe and the Middle East. Nixon also realized that a way had to be found out of Vietnam. Not only was the war costing too much money, but it was also causing deep divisions within the United States. Late in 1969 Americans were shocked to learn that Lieutenant William Calley had ordered the massacre of over 200 civilians in My Lai village in March 1968. News of the My Lai massacre seemed to confirm a growing feeling that the United States had lost its innocence in Vietnam. Massacres were committed by Nazis or Communists, not by American soldiers. The innocence of the United States was further shattered in the summer of 1970 when the country's universities exploded in protest against the war. At Kent State University in Ohio, the National Guard was sent to the campus when students began rioting. The guardsmen panicked and opened fire on the demonstrators, killing four students. Violence in South-East Asia had spawned violence in the United States.

Disillusionment with the Vietnam War grew in 1971 when the *New York Times* began publishing extracts from a secret Pentagon study that had been commissioned by Robert McNamara. The *Pentagon Papers*, as the document came to be called, revealed that President Johnson had misled Congress over the Gulf of Tonkin incident in 1964 and had drawn up plans for sending troops to Vietnam while promising the American people that troops would never be sent. Most tellingly, they showed that no plan existed for bringing the war to an end. Nixon attempted to block publication of the *Pentagon Papers*, but in the case *United States v. New York Times* (1972), the Supreme Court ruled against the administration's attempts at censorship. The American people were free to read about the destruction and lack of direction that had characterized the involvement of the United States in Vietnam.

By the late 1960s sentiment was clearly growing to bring an end to the war. The problem for both Nixon and Kissinger was to find an acceptable way to end the war. Both realized that the war could not be won at a price that Americans were willing to pay. Neither were they willing to accept the advice of Clark Clifford, a former Secretary of Defense, to declare victory and leave. Rather Nixon and Kissinger sought a 'Vietnamization' of the Vietnam War. American troops would gradually be withdrawn and replaced by South Vietnamese troops. Eventually, they reasoned, South Vietnam would be able to maintain its own independence much like South Korea.

To obtain their objectives, Nixon and Kissinger employed three different strategies. First, a secret air war against North Vietnamese supply lines in Cambodia was launched. In two years, the United States dropped four times as many bombs on Cambodia as had been dropped on Japan during the Second World War. Second, American troops were gradually withdrawn. By 1973 only 50,000 American troops remained in Vietnam. Third, Kissinger began a series of secret negotiating sessions in Paris with Le Duc Tho, a senior member of the government in Hanoi. At the meetings, Kissinger demanded that communist forces be withdrawn from South Vietnam, and the independence of the country be guaranteed. The North Vietnamese insisted on maintaining a military presence in the South and the reunification of the country under a communist government.

As was to be expected, progress at the Paris peace talks was painfully slow. Le Duc Tho frequently returned to small points which Kissinger believed had been settled, and both sides accused each other of insincerity. In an attempt to force the North Vietnamese to sign an agreement, Nixon ordered the saturation bombing of Hanoi and Haiphong on 16 December 1972. Known as the 'Christmas Bombings', Nixon's actions aroused outrage around the world, but seemed to serve their purpose. A ceasefire agreement was signed in Paris on 23 January 1973 which ended all active American involvement in the war. In fact, the 'Christmas Bombings' probably made little difference to the outcome. With Congress reassembling in January 1973, Nixon was desperate to sign an agreement before the legislature acted to cut off funds for the war.

The entry of Congress into the Vietnam War was extremely important. From the end of the Second World War to the beginning of the 1970s, Congress had generally been content to allow successive Presidents to conduct foreign policy. The seemingly unending war in Vietnam, however, acted as a spur for renewed congressional interest in foreign policy. In December 1970 Congress repealed the Gulf of Tonkin Resolution in an effort to end the war. Nixon simply ignored Congress's action. Congress then passed legislation which prohibited the use of American ground troops in Cambodia or Laos. Step by step,

Congress was putting pressure on Nixon to end the war. By the beginning of 1973, members of Congress were prepared to cut all funds for the air war.

The Paris peace agreement achieved two things. It provided for the withdrawal of American troops and the return of American POWs held in North Vietnam. It did not end the war, nor did it guarantee the security of South Vietnam. Within weeks of the departure of the last American combat troops from Vietnam on 29 March 1973 the ceasefire in Vietnam broke down. Over the next two years resistance in the South gradually crumbled before a steady onslaught by the communist forces. The end came in March 1975 when the North Vietnamese launched a major invasion of the South. On 30 April 1975 Americans watched on television as North Vietnamese tanks entered Saigon. In an ignoble conclusion to the war, those same television viewers watched thousands of South Vietnamese fight to gain entry to the US embassy in an effort to get a ride on the helicopters taking American officials to safety.

The longest, most divisive war in American history had ended. None of the goals that had been used to justify the war had been achieved. Communist governments were in control of Vietnam, Cambodia and Laos, democratic ideals seemed to be in full retreat, and faith in the military powers of American armed forces had been eroded. Abroad, allies began to question the reliability of the United States, and the country's enemies saw an opportunity to take advantage of apparent American weakness. Most Americans, however, were just glad that the war was over.

To Nixon and Kissinger the war in Vietnam was a sideshow. Both were far more concerned with the need to construct a new security arrangement which would reduce tensions in the world. To achieve such an aim they realized that they would need to forge a new relationship with both the Soviet Union and China. With the Soviet Union, the new relationship was to be based on the concept of 'detente'. The rationale of 'detente' was a recognition that both the United States and the Soviet Union had legitimate interests in the world. Recognition of each other's interests would lead to a more orderly and restrained competition between the two countries. With China, the new relationship was to be based on an ending of the diplomatic freeze that had characterized relations between the two countries since 1949. Through courting China, Nixon and Kissinger not only hoped to reduce tensions in the world, but also sought to divide the two communist superpowers.

The most serious area of competition between the United States and the Soviet Union was the race for superiority in nuclear weapons. After a rapid increase in the production of nuclear weapons in the mid-1960s, the Soviet Union had significantly reduced the superiority that the United States had previously possessed in nuclear weapons. Realizing that the nuclear superiority that the Americans had held in the 1950s was long gone, Nixon announced that sufficiency rather than superiority would be the new American strategic goal. With nuclear weapons becoming more and more expensive an unbridled race for nuclear superiority simply could not be sustained. For that reason, both Nixon and Kissinger put a great deal of effort into securing an arms control agreement with the Soviet Union. Both believed that such an arms control agreement would open the way for a more general detente with the Soviet Union.

Arms control negotiations between the United States and the Soviet Union began in 1969. Known as the Strategic Arms Limitations Talks (SALT), the negotiators eventually reached an agreement which was signed by Nixon and the Soviet leader Leonid Brezhnev in Moscow in 1972. The SALT I agreement set limits to the number of intercontinental ballistic missiles (ICBM) that each superpower could deploy, but said nothing about the number of warheads that each ICBM could carry. Nor did SALT I prohibit the development of new weapons systems, although it did place strict limits on the construction of anti-ballistic missile systems (ABMS). The latter was intended to ensure that each country's population would be hostage to a strategic missile attack. As mutually assured destruction (MAD) would be the only outcome of a nuclear war, both the United States and the Soviet Union would have a vested interest in avoiding war.

SALT I did not end the arms race. Both the United States and the Soviet Union continued to add warheads to their nuclear arsenals. In 1973 the United States had 6,000 warheads, and the Soviet Union 2,500 warheads. By 1977 the United States had 10,000 warheads, and the Soviet Union 4,000 warheads. If SALT I did not end the arms race, however, it did open the way for a more general detente between the two countries. At the Moscow Summit, Nixon signed a number of trade agreements with Leonid Brezhnev. The most important of these was an arrangement whereby the United States sold huge quantities of wheat to the Soviet Union. In 1972 almost one-quarter of the wheat produced in the United States was sold to the Soviets. Despite being subsidized by the American government, such wheat sales helped reduce the balance of payments deficit that the United States was beginning to suffer.

Elsewhere, detente spawned a number of symbolic acts. In June 1972, Nixon signed the Berlin Agreement which provided for improved communications between the four sectors of Berlin and American recognition of East Germany. Two years later, the United States established formal diplomatic relations with East Germany. In recognizing and establishing formal diplomatic relations with East Germany, the United States was effectively abandoning its policy of working towards the establishment of a united Germany. American recognition of the borders of other East European states came when Nixon signed the Helsinki Accords in 1972. The Helsinki Accords guaranteed the territorial integrity of the European states that had been created at the end of the Second World War, and also committed all the signatories to the defence of human rights.

Although detente represented a significant change in American policy towards the Soviet Union, a far more radical change in the foreign policy of the United States was signalled when Nixon announced in July 1971 that he would be visiting China. Since 1949 the United States had refused to recognize the communist government of China. It had preferred, instead, to regard Chiang-Kai-shek's exiled nationalist government on the island of Taiwan (Formosa) as the legitimate government of China. That it should have been Nixon who would begin the process of changing such a policy was ironic. Nixon had condemned the Truman Administration for 'losing China' in 1949, and had been associated with the policy of non-recognition thoughout his career. As President, however, Nixon realized that the policy of non-recognition had little to recommend it. He also realized that ending the diplomatic isolation of China presented him with an opportunity to do something 'historic'.

Nixon's visit to China took place in February 1972. For a week American television viewers watched their President as he visited the Great Wall of China, and met with Zhou Enlai and Mao Zedong. A joint communique, issued from Shanghai, reported that the United States and China had agreed to scientific and cultural exchanges. Both countries also agreed to work towards the normalization of relations. As a first step, 'liaison offices' were established in Washington DC and Peking in 1973 to serve as unofficial embassies. Formal recognition of China did not occur until December 1978 when President Jimmy

Carter announced that he was establishing full diplomatic relations with China. At the same time Carter abrogated the mutual defence treaty between the United States and Taiwan.

The efforts by Nixon and Kissinger to seek both detente with the Soviet Union and rapprochement with China were the most dramatic developments in American foreign policy during the early 1970s. Less dramatic, but perhaps of greater testimony to the foreign policy skills of Nixon and Kissinger, was their response to events in the Middle East following the Yom Kippur War of 1973. When Egypt and Syria attacked Israel on 6 October 1973 they enjoyed initial success, but then started losing ground as the Israelis counter-attacked using newly supplied American weapons. In retaliation for American support of Israel the Arab oil states, led by Saudia Arabia, imposed an effective embargo on oil shipments to the United States and Western Europe. Negotiating a ceasefire and an end to the oil embargo became a top priority for the Nixon Administration.

Resolving the crisis in the Middle East took considerable skill. First, Kissinger had to arrange for a ceasefire. He then had to arrange for a disengagement of the various armies. To achieve such ends Kissinger engaged in 'step-by-step' diplomacy. Deliberately ignoring questions such as the fate of the Palestinians, Kissinger flew from capital to capital in the Middle East in an effort to resolve smaller questions such as the fate of each country's prisoners of war. Success came slowly. On 18 January 1974 he persuaded the Egyptians and Israelis to disengage their forces. Finally, on 31 May 1974 he managed to secure a ceasefire and troop disengagement agreement between Israel and Syria.

Engineering a ceasefire in the Middle East was the last major foreign policy achievement of the Nixon Administration. On 9 August 1974 Nixon resigned as evidence of his involvement in the Watergate scandal became public. The foreign policy objectives of the Nixon Administration, however, continued to be followed by President Gerald Ford who retained Henry Kissinger as Secretary of State. Seeking to further detente with the Soviet Union, Ford attended a summit with Leonid Brezhnev at Vladivostok in late 1974 at which the foundations for a new arms control agreement were laid. In the Middle East, Kissinger continued his shuttle diplomacy and eventually reached an agreement between Egypt and Israel. Under the terms of this agreement, Israel promised to return to Egypt most of the Sinai Desert captured in the Six Day War of 1967, and both countries agreed to rely on negotiations rather than war to settle disagreements in the future.

President Ford's defeat in the presidential election of 1976 finally ended the Nixon–Kissinger era. Just what that era achieved, however, has been a source of great debate. Supporters of Nixon and Kissinger have suggested that the two men transformed the United States' relationship with the Soviet Union, established contacts with China, secured the withdrawal of American troops from Vietnam and helped promote stability in the Middle East. Critics, on the other hand, have challenged the assumption that relations between the United States and the Soviet Union really changed with the advent of detente. They stressed the fact that Nixon had spent thirty years of his political career blocking contacts with China, prolonged the withdrawal from Vietnam for four years and did little to resolve the basic problems in the Middle East. They also argued, with some justice, that Nixon's policy of detente, with its dilution of the ideological underpinning of American foreign policy, was confusing. For a quarter of a century the Truman Doctrine had acted as a yardstick of American interests abroad. It was now subordinated to the geopolitical calculations of the White House inner circle. Whatever the truth of these different claims, one thing is clear. By 1976 the American people had had enough of the 'realpolitik' of the Nixon–Kissinger era. Idealism and not expediency was demanded.

The man to whom Americans turned in the wake of the Nixon–Kissinger era was Jimmy Carter. In his Inaugural Address Carter offered a view of the United States' role in the world which stood in sharp contrast to that of his predecessors. He declared that his ultimate goal was the elimination of nuclear weapons, and made a firm commitment to the defence of human rights. Events were to prove both goals to be impractical. There was to be no reduction in the nuclear arsenal of the United States during the Carter Administration, and the emphasis on human rights not only damaged America's relations with allies such as Argentina, South Korea, Nicaragua and Iran, but also caused resentment in the Soviet Union.

Although Carter's idealistic approach to foreign affairs would later prove to be disastrous, he did enjoy some success at the beginning of his presidency. First, he managed to secure Senate ratification of the Panama Canal Treaty. In doing so he managed to overcome considerable conservative opposition to the idea of returning control of the Panama Canal Zone to Panama. Second, he acted quickly to exploit the diplomatic opportunities created when President Anwar el-Sadat of Egypt flew to Tel Aviv in December 1977 to address the Knesset, the Israeli Parliament. In September 1978 Carter invited Sadat and the Israeli Prime Minister, Menachem Begin, to meet with him at the Presidential retreat at Camp David, Maryland. After two weeks of negotiations the foundations of an eventual peace treaty were laid. In return for an Israeli withdrawal from the Sinai the Egyptians would recognise Israel and establish diplomatic and economic relations with their old enemy.

What became known as the 'Camp David Accords' were Carter's greatest foreign policy triumph. Any satisfaction that Carter might have felt soon disappeared, however, as other aspects of his foreign policy began to turn sour. Relations with the Soviet Union declined, and most humbling of all, events in Iran were to demonstrate clearly to the world the limits of American power. By the end of the decade the foreign policy of the United States would be in disarray, and Jimmy Carter would be out of office.

The tone of Soviet–American relations in the first years of Carter's Administration was set by Cyrus Vance, the Secretary of State. Vance urged a new approach towards the Soviet Union based upon 'positive incentives' rather than a policy of containment. Within 24 hours of taking office, Carter announced that he was withdrawing all American nuclear weapons from South Korea as the first of these 'positive incentives'. When the Soviets did not respond to Carter's action it became evident that a policy based on 'positive incentives' was not going to work. As the man most closely associated with that policy, Vance's authority within the administration gradually declined. Carter increasingly began to rely upon the advice of his National Security Adviser, Zbigniew Brzezinski. Brzezinski made powerful arguments for not trusting the Soviets, and his influence led to a perceptible hardening in Carter's attitude towards them.

At the outset of his term in office, Carter placed great emphasis on signing a SALT II treaty which would reduce the chances of nuclear war. The possibility of securing an early agreement on nuclear weapons was lost, however, as Carter became increasingly concerned about signs of Soviet aggression in Angola and Ethiopia. The Soviets themselves became increasingly resentful towards Carter's support for dissidents in the Soviet Union and his technique of linking SALT talks to human rights. As a result, Carter and Brezhnev did not meet until June 1979 to sign the SALT II treaty. As with SALT I the new agreement did not stop the arms race. Rather than freezing nuclear weapons and delivery systems at their current levels, the treaty set upper limits to which both sides could build. The treaty limited each country to 2,400 delivery systems, but placed no limit on the number of warheads those delivery systems could carry.

As a treaty, SALT II was criticized from both ends of the political spectrum. Liberals argued that it did little to halt the proliferation of nuclear weapons, and conservatives charged that it gave away too much to the Soviet Union. With opposition from both the left and right, many observers questioned whether SALT II would pass the Senate. The question of ratification rapidly became moot, however, when the Soviet army invaded Afghanistan in December 1979. Reacting to the invasion, Carter suspended SALT II.

The Soviet invasion of Afghanistan on Christmas Day 1979 came as a shock to Carter who viewed the move as the first step in a Soviet plan to dominate the Persian Gulf. In addition to suspending SALT II, Carter ordered a halt to grain sales to the Soviet Union and urged a boycott of the 1980 Olympic Games in Moscow. Fearing a threat to the West's oil supplies, Carter also defined the Persian Gulf as an area of strategic importance to the United States. Any Soviet attack on the region would be resisted, with military force if necessary, by the United States.

For a man who had assumed office in 1976 with the aim of reducing tension between the United States and the Soviet Union, Carter had achieved very little. If anything, relations between the two superpowers in 1980 were worse than they were in 1976. Part of the blame for the deterioration in relations lay with the Soviets, who viewed Carter's efforts at friendship as signs of weakness which they could exploit. Blame for the increase in tension, however, also lay with Carter whose inexperience in foreign affairs often led him to overreact to events. Unlike Nixon and Kissinger, Carter never seemed to be in control of events. Rather, events tended to carry him along.

Carter's inability to control events was graphically illustrated during the Iranian hostage crisis. The crisis began on 16 January 1979 when the Shah of Iran, a long-time ally of the United States, was overthrown in a revolution. Two weeks later, the Ayatollah Khomeini, a Moslem religious leader who had been in exile in Paris, returned to Iran to become the *de facto* ruler of the country. Although Khomeini denounced both the Americans and the Soviets, his hatred of the United States struck a chord in those Iranians who remembered the CIA-sponsored overthrow of Iran's Mossadeq government in 1953. Other

Iranians recalled that SAVAK, the Shah's secret police force, had also been trained by the CIA. Few Iranians believed that the United States would abandon the Shah, and feared another CIA-sponsored coup. Such fears grew when the Shah was allowed to enter the United States in October 1979 in order to undergo treatment for cancer.

On 4 November 1979 a mob stormed the American Embassy in Teheran and seized the diplomats and staff inside. Khomeini condoned the action and stated that the American hostages would only be released if the Shah was returned to Iran. The seizure of the embassy was clearly a violation of international law, but there was little that Carter could do. He appealed to the United Nations, froze all Iranian assets in the United States, and urged the United States' allies to boycott Iran. When none of these actions proved successful, Carter finally ordered a rescue attempt by American commandos. The military operation on the 25 April 1980 was a disaster. Long before the commandos got anywhere near Teheran, Carter was forced to abort the mission because of equipment failures. Eight Americans died when a helicoptor collided with a transport plane in the Iranian desert. A more graphic illustration of the reduced stature of the United States would have been difficult to imagine.

The Iranian crisis spelled the end of any chance that Carter might have had to win re-election. Every night American television reported on the crisis, and reminded the viewers of the apparent powerlessness of their country. Carter's Republican opponent in the election, Ronald Reagan, was the natural beneficiary of this sense of impotence. He did not find it difficult to convince voters that the Iranian crisis was the outcome of a leadership that not only was indecisive but also cavalier with the nation's security. The end of the hostages' ordeal finally came on Carter's last morning in office when he authorized the release of $8 billion worth of Iranian assets as a ransom for the hostages. A plane carrying the hostages left Teheran for Algiers seconds after Ronald Reagan finished his Inaugural Address.

Further reading

Zbigniew Brzezinski, *Power and Principle* (New York, 1983).

Raymond Garthoff, *Detente and Confrontation* (Washington, D.C., 1985).

Seymour M. Hersh, *The Price of Power* (New York, 1983).

Gareth Porter, *A Peace Denied* (Bloomington, 1975).

Harvey Starr, *Henry Kissinger* (Lexington, KY, 1984).

Cyrus Vance, *Hard Choices* (New York, 1983).

12

The new Republican era, 1981-1990

By 1980 the United States appeared to be in the middle of a deep and profound crisis. The economy was plagued by high levels of unemployment, rising rates of inflation and high interest rates. Inflation averaged between 12 and 13 per cent for most of 1980, reaching a peak of 18 per cent in one month, unemployment stood at 7.5 per cent and interest rates were at an all-time high of 20 per cent. The social programmes of the 1960s and early 1970s were largely discredited. Poverty, social deprivation and crime remained only too evident in most American cities. Abroad, the country seemed to be in full retreat. Soviet expansionism in Africa and Asia, most notably in Afghanistan, fuelled criticism of detente, and the Iranian hostage crisis was for many a perfect symbol of American impotence. A country which had appeared almost omnipotent in 1945 was made only too aware of its apparent shortcomings in 1980 as American newscasters finished their broadcasts each evening by reminding their viewers of the number of days that the hostages had been held captive in Teheran.

The apparently irreversible decline of the United States spawned a number of challenges to the public philosophy which had dominated American life since the New Deal. Economists began to dispute the efficacy of Keynesian techniques of demand management as a means of controlling inflation and unemployment. Monetarists, such as Milton Friedman of the University of Chicago, argued that inflation was not caused by excess demand as claimed by Keynes, but by too rapid growth in the money supply. Supply-side economists like Arthur Laffer of the University of Southern California, argued that economic growth could only be obtained by rewarding enterprise. This would involve cutting taxes and reducing government regulation of the economy. Other intellectuals challenged the very premises of the welfare liberalism that had slowly developed in the United States since the New Deal. Neo-conservatives such as Irving Kristol, editor of

Public Interest, and Norman Podhoretz, editor of *Commentary*, argued that the Great Society programmes had been a disaster. Not only
were they very expensive, but they were also counter-productive.
Rather than eliminating poverty, Kristol and Podhoretz contended,
the programmes of the Great Society had made the situation worse by
creating a dependency upon welfare which was very difficult to break.
In the view of the neo-conservatives, there were simply some problems
within society which were beyond the scope of any government
to cure.

Neo-conservatism, monetarism and supply-side economics may be
viewed as an intellectual reaction to an apparently discredited public
philosophy. The main arena for the discussion of such ideas were the
universities and the intellectual journals of New York. Concern over the
effects of the policies of the 1960s and 1970s, however, could also be
found at the grass-roots level. Rising crime rates, the spread of
pornography, an increase in the rate of divorce, together with Supreme
Court decisions which legalized abortion and prohibited prayer in
schools, spawned a number of groups committed to reversing what
were perceived to be attacks on the family and on the American way of
life. Commonly identified as the New Right, these groups included
religious organizations like the Moral Majority, political organizations
such as the National Conservative Political Action Committee and
various single-issue groups of which perhaps the most vocal were the
so-called 'pro-life' or anti-abortion groups. Their constituencies were
the white, upper-working class and lower-middle class groups, who felt
most threatened by the developments of the last two decades.

The person who was to gain most from the growing conservative
tide in the United States was Ronald Reagan. A former actor and
two-term governor of California, Reagan had previously made two
attempts to secure the Republican nomination for President. He had
established a reputation for patriotic nationalism and for his advocacy
of retrenchment in government. In 1968 he lost a last-minute attempt
to win the nomination, and in 1976 narrowly failed to wrest it from
Gerald Ford. By 1980, however, events seemed to be conspiring to
propel him to the White House. Although George Bush posed a threat
to Reagan in the early stages of the campaign, the contest was all but
over by March. Reagan's communicative skills, together with his appeal
to the powerful conservative elements within the Republican Party,
were sufficient to secure him the nomination. By fashioning a campaign
which would appeal to the increasing number of Americans who were

disillusioned with the policies of the past, he would go on to win the presidency.

Jimmy Carter's attempt to retain the presidency was in trouble from the start. A strong effort from Edward Kennedy to wrest the nomination from Carter created conflict and divisions within the Democratic Party. The Iranian hostage crisis undermined Carter's image as a strong leader, and the poor performance of the economy cast a shadow over the efficacy of Democratic policies. In perhaps the most important moment of the campaign Reagan alluded to the problems that the economy was causing. At the end of the final television debate in Cleveland, on 28 October 1980, Reagan asked the audience: 'Are you better off than you were four years ago?' It was an effective way of focusing the mind of the electorate upon the record of the Carter Administration. Beset with domestic and foreign problems, Carter had no means of countering Reagan's campaign, and defeat in the November election was almost inevitable. As it turned out, Reagan won nearly 51 per cent of the popular vote to Carter's 41 per cent, with John Anderson, an independent candidate, gaining most of the rest of the vote. It was hardly an impressive victory. In terms of the electoral college, however, Reagan's victory seemed overwhelming. Reagan won 489 electoral votes to Carter's 49. Carter carried a mere six states, together with the District of Columbia. With the landslide in the electoral college obscuring the results of the popular vote, Reagan moved quickly to assert that he had received a mandate for change.

The type of change which President Reagan wanted to bring about had been hinted at during the election campaign. At the end of the first television debate he had declared: 'I would like to have a great crusade today. And it would be to take government off the backs of the great people of this country and turn you loose again to do the things that I know you can do so well, because you did them and made this country great.' The theme that government was a cause and not a solution to the problems facing society was further developed in President Reagan's First Inaugural Address. Reagan promised the American people 'a new beginning'. In words which echoed the work of the supply-side economists he attacked a 'tax system which penalizes successful achievement and keeps us from maintaining full productivity'. Echoes of President Eisenhower's Farewell Address could also be heard in Reagan's concern that budget deficits were 'mortgaging our future and our children's future for the temporary convenience of the present'. Perhaps even a few echoes of President Franklin D. Roosevelt's First

Inaugural Address could be heard when Reagan concluded his speech by calling upon Americans 'To believe in ourselves and to believe ... that together we can and will resolve the problems which confront us'. Unlike Roosevelt, however, Reagan believed that the problems facing the United States could not be solved by government. His Inaugural Address defined an agenda of tax cuts, budget cuts and a reduction in the role and size of government. It was a clear declaration of war upon the philosophy of the New Deal and Great Society.

The first shots in the war against the legacy of the New Deal and the Great Society were fired within the first few months of President Reagan assuming office. Two measures were submitted to Congress for consideration. The first measure was designed to cut taxes, and the second to reduce the level of government spending. In the past such measures would have had little chance of gaining the approval of Congress, but in 1981 circumstances worked to the advantage of President Reagan. Not only had the Republicans gained control of the Senate in the 1980 elections, but they had also made sufficient gains in the House of Representatives to ensure that a conservative coalition of Republicans and Southern Democrats would have a majority. When combined with a feeling that President Reagan had received an electoral mandate for his economic policies, such arithmetic ensured that the economic proposals of the President would be treated sympathetically. Both of the measures submitted to Congress were, in fact, passed. The Economic Recovery Tax Act (1981) cut personal taxes by 25 per cent across the board over a period of thirty-three months, reduced the top rate of federal income tax from 70 to 50 per cent for 1982 and lowered the rate of capital gains tax from 28 per cent to 20 per cent. In total, the tax cuts contained in this Act amounted to $737 billion over five years. Meanwhile, the Omnibus Budget and Reconciliation Act (1981) reduced the level of federal spending for 1982 by $35.2 billion. Budget cuts were aimed at health, education and housing programmes, urban aid, food stamps and school meals. While the administration sought to cut back on welfare spending, it did not want to compromise the national security. Defence spending for 1982 was increased by $12.3 billion.

During the 1980 election campaign Ronald Reagan had consistently argued that his economic proposals would lead to a balanced budget. He argued that the tax cuts would stimulate economic growth and reduce levels of unemployment. Such changes would reduce the amount of social security which the government would have to pay and at the same time would bring more people into the tax net. Such arguments were dismissed as 'voodoo economics' at the time by George Bush, who was competing with Reagan for the Republican nomination. What is clear, however, is that the projections of a balanced budget made by Reagan were predicated upon an extremely optimistic set of forecasts about the future performance of the American economy. In fact, the economy continued to perform poorly in 1982. Although the rate of inflation fell from more than 12 per cent in 1980 to a mere 4 per cent by the end of 1982, the level of unemployment rose to its highest level since the Great Depression. By December 1982 the rate of unemployment in the United States stood at 10.8 per cent. With unemployment at such a high level, the arguments that tax cuts would produce a balanced budget seemed particularly misplaced. Not only did more people require social security but the number of people paying taxes fell. The result was a large budget deficit.

When President Reagan assumed office in 1981 the budget deficit of the United States was $79 million or 2.7 per cent of the country's Gross National Product (GNP). After one year of 'Reaganomics' the budget deficit was $128 billion or 4.1 per cent of GNP. Over the next two years the budget deficit continued to grow despite the fact that the unemployment rate had fallen. The worsening deficit was caused by the increases in defence spending, which Reagan repeatedly espoused. Congress also restored many of the spending cuts of 1981. By 1984 the budget deficit was $203 billion or 5.7 per cent of GNP. The large size of these deficits meant that almost as much debt was accumulated in the first four years of the Reagan Administration as had been accumulated in the previous two hundred years of the country's existence. In 1981 the national debt of the United States stood at just under $800 billion. By 1984 the national debt stood at $1.5 trillion.

Concern about the size of the budget deficit dominated the political agenda of the United States in the years after 1981. Both President Reagan and Congress accused each other of irresponsible behaviour. While President Reagan criticized Congress for failing to cut spending on domestic programmes, members of Congress criticized President Reagan for his refusal to reduce spending on defence. Neither branch of government countenanced raising taxes as an alternative method of reducing the deficit. Finally, in an effort to break the impasse over the budget deficit Congress passed the Gramm-Rudman-Hollings Act in 1985. The original intention of this law was to mandate automatic cuts in government programmes until the deficit was erased. Political pressures, however, led to programmes such as social security, veterans' pensions, Medicaid and food stamps being exempted from the cuts required by Gramm-Rudman-Hollings. As a result, the budget deficit was hardly dented. In 1989 the deficit was still close to $150 billion.

The consequences of large budget deficits were profound. On the one hand they helped to fuel the economic recovery which the United States enjoyed from 1983 to mid-1988. For almost five years the United States enjoyed economic growth, low rates of inflation and an unemployment rate below 6 per cent. On the other hand the need to finance such deficits generated certain problems. First, the high interest rates that were necessary to attract sufficient funds to meet the government's borrowing requirement discouraged business investment. With business investment being necessary for future economic growth, one of the long-term consequences of the large deficits may well be reduced economic growth in the 1990s. Second, high interest rates in the United States attracted unprecedented levels of foreign investment to the United States. In 1986 the United States became the world's largest debtor nation as foreign investment in the United States exceeded the level of American investment in other countries for the first time since the First World War. One result of this was an over-valued dollar which made American goods more difficult to export and led to a worsening of the trade deficit. Third, the need to pay interest on all this debt has consumed an increasing proportion of the national income of the United States. By 1989 just under 6 per cent of the nation's GNP went towards paying interest on the national debt.

Although President Reagan was unable to achieve his goal of a balanced budget, somewhat ironically, the deficit helped to promote his goal of reducing the power of the federal government. With the need to reduce spending dominating the political agenda in Washington DC, Americans began to look to state and local governments for solutions to their problems. The result was a renewed vitality in levels of government below the federal level. Instead of relying upon initiatives from the federal government, individual states and cities sought to find their own solutions to the problems caused by poverty, crime and drugs. For the first time since the New Deal power began to shift away from Washington DC and back to the state capitals. In that sense, the budget deficit had succeeded in bringing about results which earlier initiatives such as President Nixon's 'New Federalism' had failed to achieve. Expectations about what could be achieved from Washington DC had finally been lowered by the fact that the federal government was bankrupt.

For most Americans, the size of the budget deficit was unimportant. Low inflation, falling rates of unemployment and sustained economic growth created an environment which benefited the Republicans. Using the slogan 'America's Back Again' Reagan ran a campaign in 1984 which stressed the renewed prosperity of the United States. The result was a landslide for President Reagan who secured 59 per cent of the popular vote and lost only Minnesota and the District of Columbia. In 1988, George Bush, who had served eight years as Reagan's Vice-President, ran a similar campaign to win election to the presidency. Identifying himself closely with the policies of the Reagan era, Bush easily defeated Michael Dukakis, the governor of Massachusetts. Uncertainty held no attractions.

Although much of the electoral success of Ronald Reagan and George Bush may be attributed to economic factors, events in the foreign arena also played into their hands. From the outset, President Reagan sought to restore American prestige and authority around the world. The new administration took a tough line with the Soviet Union, focused considerable attention on events in Central America and ordered a dramatic build-up in arms. Policies which had been advocated by President Carter, and even by President Nixon, were ridiculed and abandoned. Carter's human rights policy was rejected. Detente as understood by Nixon and Carter was replaced by a new policy of containment. Weapons which had been cancelled by Carter were put into production. For all his determination to restore American authority, however, Reagan soon discovered that he was unable to impose his will upon the world. Military strength alone was not sufficient to control events in the 1980s. Reagan was fortunate in that most events seemed to go his way. Unlike Carter, he was simply lucky.

At the outset of his first term in office, President Reagan was preoccupied with events in Central America. Arguing that the Sandinista Government of Nicaragua was supplying weapons to left wing guerillas in El Salvador, Reagan sought not only to stop the flow of weapons into El Salvador, but also to overthrow the Sandinistas. In the opinion of the administration, the threat posed by the Sandinistas and the guerillas in El Salvador was twofold. First, it was suggested that Nicaragua would become another Cuba. It was already being used as a base for the export of revolution throughout the region. If the pattern continued the Soviet Union could gain a foothold there. Second, it was suggested that a communist victory in El Salvador would lead to a massive flight of refugees from Central America into the United States. With the country unable to cope with an influx of refugees from Mexico, the spectre of millions of Central Americans crossing the Rio Grande caused consternation in the White House.

Reagan's fears about events in Central America were not shared in Congress. Few members of Congress agreed with the administration's analysis of events, and most members of the general public were fearful of becoming involved in another Vietnam. Opposition in Congress meant that Reagan's options were severely limited. Congress did agree to limited financial aid to the government of El Salvador, but tied such aid to improvements in that government's human rights record. Requests by President Reagan for money to support the 'Contra' guerillas fighting against the Sandinista government were also treated with scepticism in Congress. The result was stalemate. President Reagan was unable to persuade his critics in Congress of the efficacy of his policies, and those congressional critics were unable to persuade Reagan to change his policies.

In an attempt to break the stalemate on Central America, President Reagan came very close to entangling himself in a scandal similar to Watergate. When Congress passed the Boland Amendment in 1984, which prohibited further military support for the Contras, Reagan responded by devising a number of means to circumvent the spirit, if not the letter, of the law. Contributions for the Contras were solicited from private citizens, the CIA continued to support the Contras, and in the basement of the White House Colonel Oliver North, a member of the NSC staff, devised a plan to raise funds for the Contras. North's plan was to sell arms to the Iranians, and use the profits from such arms sales to finance the Contras. Such a plan also promised to facilitate the release of American citizens held hostage by Muslim extremists in Beirut.

News of the Iran–Contra link broke in late 1986 when a Beirut newspaper published some of the details of the arms sales to Iran. During the weeks that followed, the scale of North's operation became clear as Congress and the media began investigating the arms sales to Iran. On 25 November 1986, National Security Advisor John Poindexter was forced to resign, and Colonel Oliver North was relieved of his duties. Reagan denied direct knowledge of the affair and appointed a three-man commission under former Senator John Tower to investigate the scandal. The Report of the Tower Commission, published in early 1987, placed much of the responsibility for the scandal on the loose management style of the Reagan White House. The Tower Report made the resignation of Donald Regan, President Reagan's Chief of Staff, inevitable.

In reality, the Iran–Contra affair highlighted more than management problems in the Reagan White House. Most importantly, the affair highlighted the tension generated by a system of government which gave the President responsibility for the conduct of foreign policy, but only half the power necessary to meet such a responsibility. Denied support in Congress, Reagan sought to conduct a clandestine foreign policy using the NSC and CIA. That he was able to survive the disclosure of such a clandestine policy was testimony both to Reagan's political skill and his luck. Reagan moved quickly to distance himself from the Iran–Contra scandal by suggesting ignorance of what was happening in the White House, and Congress was unable to impeach a popular President so close to the 1988 elections.

If President Reagan was unable to turn back communism in Nicaragua, he was far more successful in defeating communism on the Caribbean island of Grenada. In October 1983, a military coup led by General Hudson Austin overthrew and killed Maurice Bishop, the Prime Minister of Grenada. Austin promised to be even more radical than Bishop, who had caused concern in Washington DC by entering into military agreements with other communist governments and allowing Cuban construction workers to build a new airfield, and prompted the United States to intervene. On 25 October 1983, Reagan ordered 1,900 marines to invade Grenada and depose Austin. The Cuban workers fought back, but could not hope to defeat the American forces, and a new government was installed on the Island. Countries throughout the world condemned the American action as an example of 'gunboat diplomacy', but for Reagan it was a triumph. It showed that he could be tough and added to his popularity. More importantly, the invasion diverted attention from events in Lebanon.

The United States became directly involved in Lebanon following the Israeli invasion of that country in June 1982. Israeli troops quickly pushed PLO troops out of southern Lebanon, and by late July had the Palestinians trapped in Beirut. In August 1982, the Israelis began to shell PLO strongholds in Beirut. The destruction that the Israelis wrought led to demands for the United States to negotiate a ceasefire.

Reacting to public pressure, President Reagan sent a special ambassador, Philip Habib to negotiate a settlement. After weeks of effort Habib finally managed to produce an agreement which involved French, Italian and American supervision of the withdrawal of the PLO from Beirut. Following an evacuation of the PLO the trilateral force was withdrawn. Upon the removal of the PLO soldiers from Beirut and the withdrawal of the trilateral force, the Israeli army moved into the city. With Israeli soldiers looking on, Christian militiamen entered the Palestinian refugee camps and slaughtered hundreds of women and children.

The slaughter in the Palestinian refugee camps forced the return of the trilateral force as 'peacekeepers'. Lacking sufficient numbers to deter aggression, however, the 'peacekeepers' soon became targets. Muslim militiamen kept the US marines under constant fire, and forced the Americans to respond by shelling and bombing Muslim positions. On 23 October 1983 a suicide truck loaded with explosives was driven into the Marine headquarters and 241 Americans were killed. Although Reagan responded with a promise to find and punish those responsible, in reality he was powerless. In January 1984 he began preparations for withdrawal, and on 7 February 1984 announced that the Marines would be 'redeployed' to warships offshore. Like President Carter in Iran, Reagan had discovered that being commander-in-chief of the most powerful armed forces in the world was not sufficient to bring about a favourable outcome to events in the Middle East.

In his dealings with Central America and the Middle East, President Reagan was hampered not only by an inability to control events, but also by a lack of clear goals. No such lack of clarity, however, impinged upon Reagan's relations with the Soviet Union. Reagan's goals were unambivalent. He wanted peace, arms control, good trade relations and more generally, a meaningful detente. Few Americans disagreed with such goals. Disagreement arose over the best means of achieving such ends.

At the beginning of his term of office, President Reagan sought to achieve his goals by resurrecting the rhetoric of the Cold War. In a Press Conference held in February 1981 Reagan declared that the leaders of the Soviet Union had 'reserved unto themselves the right to commit any crime, to lie, to cheat' in order to gain 'world domination through world rule of communist states'. Such rhetoric reached its peak in March 1983 when Reagan depicted the Soviet Union as an 'evil empire' and 'the focus of evil in the modern world'. In making such accusations, Reagan was rejecting Carter's conception of detente in which the United States sought to accommodate the Soviet Union. Reagan believed that the only way to deal with the Soviet Union was from a position of strength. If the Soviets perceived any weakness, they would simply take advantage. To build up the strength of the United States, Reagan ordered a massive increase in defence spending. Reagan calculated that if the Soviets did not match these increases, it would give the United States a decisive edge. If the Soviets did try to keep up, the escalating costs would cause severe damage to their economy. Accordingly, in the first three years of his presidency, spending on defence increased by forty per cent in real terms.

For a while, it was not clear how Reagan's calculations would resolve themselves. Predictably, the United States' increase in defence spending merely sparked off a corresponding increase in arms expenditure in the Soviet Union. Events, however, were soon to play into Reagan's hands. In March 1985, a new Soviet leader, Mikhail Gorbachev, came to power. Gorbachev had a radically different agenda than had his predecessors. He recognized that the Soviet Union would need to restructure its economy if it was to survive into the twenty-first century. Since the Soviet Union spent nearly twice the proportion of its GNP on defence than the United States did, Gorbachev wanted to divert investment from armaments to consumer industries. Reductions in defence spending could only be sustained if tensions abroad were eased. His policy of *perestroika* called for initiatives and reforms on all fronts. Some co-operation from the United States was indispensable. The stage was set for the first meeting of an American President and a Soviet leader for six years.

Reagan and Gorbachev met in Geneva in November 1985 and signed a number of agreements on scientific and cultural exchanges. Agreement on arms control was blocked, however, by President Reagan's refusal to restrict development of his Strategic Defense Initiative (SDI). Announced in 1983, SDI (or 'Star Wars' as it was popularly called) was a plan to construct a defence system in space which would be capable of shooting down incoming Soviet missiles. Reagan's adherence to SDI also meant that a second summit, held in Reykjavik in October 1986, failed to reach agreement. Although no progress was made towards an agreement on limiting strategic weapons at Reykjavik, the two leaders did agree to speed up negotiations on the reduction of intermediate range nuclear forces (INF) based in Europe. In December 1987 the two leaders signed a treaty which eliminated intermediate range nuclear missiles in Europe. While this did not significantly reduce the total number of warheads held by each power, its symbolic importance was enormous. For the first time, the two superpowers had agreed to eliminate an entire range of nuclear weapons.

Important though the INF Treaty was, its significance for American foreign policy was dwarfed by the changes in Eastern Europe which took place in 1989. Encouraged by Gorbachev, a wave of reform swept through Eastern Europe in late 1989. In Poland, Hungary, Bulgaria, Czechoslovakia and East Germany, the communist governments which had held power since the end of the Second World War were forced to loosen their grip on power. Most symbolically, the Berlin Wall was breached as East Germany was forced to allow free movement to the West. The division of Europe had begun in Germany. It seemed as if it would end in Germany too.

By the beginning of the 1990s the world which had been crafted by Roosevelt had started to collapse. In terms of domestic policy, the prominent position of the federal government had been undermined by the size of the budget deficit. Although a return to the political system of pre-1930 America was unlikely, the individual states had begun to re-establish themselves as important sources of political initiatives. In terms of foreign policy, the changes of the late 1980s were equally dramatic. With extraordinary change in Eastern Europe and the Soviet Union, the policy of containment appeared to be redundant. The United States' national security policy had been built on the assumption that Europe was its first line of defence. If the division of Europe were to end and the two superpowers no longer referred to the ideological underpinnings of their rivalry, then the security arrangements that had operated for forty years were becoming redundant. And if they were not redundant, it became difficult to understand the purpose they served. Slowly, but surely, the unhappy and uncertain settlement of the Second World War was being undone.

Further reading

Robert Dallek, *Ronald Reagan* (Cambridge, Mass., 1990).

John Devaney, *President Ronald Reagan* (New York, 1990).

Dilys M. Hill, Raymond A. Moore and Phil Williams (eds.), *The Reagan Presidency* (New York, 1989).

David Stockman, *The Triumph of Politics* (New York, 1986).

George Sullivan, *Ronald Reagan* (New York, 1985).

Gary Wills, *Reagan's America* (New York, 1988).

Index

Afghanistan, 140, 143
African Americans, *see* blacks
Agricultural Adjustment Administration, 10, 15
Alexander v. Holmes County Board of Education (1969), 122
Alliance for Progress, 111
Amerasia, 46
American Liberty League, 12
Anderson, John, 145
Angola, 139
Arbenz, Jacobo, 85-6
Armas, Castillo, 86
Atlantic Charter, 31
atomic bomb, 34-5, 54

Ball, George, 109
Bay of Pigs, 106-8
Begin, Menachem, 139
Beirut, 151-2
Berle, Adolph A., 18
Berlin
    allied rights, 90
    blockade (1948-49), 60-1
    crisis of 1961, 108-9
    dismantling of Berlin Wall, 154
    East German agreement under Nixon, 136
Bishop, Maurice, 151
Bissell, Richard, 107
Blackmun, Harry, 123
blacks, 1, 27, 39, 42-4, 94-7, 99-102, 116

Boland Amendment (1984), 150
bonus marchers, 6
Bowles, Chester, 108
Brezhnev, Leonid, 135, 137
Brown v. Board of Education of Topeka, Kansas, 44, 71-3
Brownlow Committee (Committee on Administration of the Federal Government), 18
Brzezinski, Zbigniew, 139
Bundy, McGeorge, 94
Bush, George, 144, 147, 149
Byrd, Harry, F., 72
Byrnes, James F., 54-5

Calley, William, 132
Cambodia, 133-4
Carmichael, Stokely, 101
Carson, Rachel, 124
Carter, Jimmy
    arms limitation, 139-40
    economic policy, 128-9
    human rights, 138, 149
    Iran hostage crisis, 140-1, 152
    Middle East, 138-9
    Panama Canal treaty, 138
    presidential election (1976) 127-8
    presidential election (1980), 144-5
    relations with China, 136-7
Castro, Fidel, 85, 104, 107-8
Causwell, Harold, 123

Central Intelligence Agency (CIA), 85, 107, 140, 150
Chambers, Whittaker, 46
Chiang-Kai-Shek, 55, 60, 63, 84, 136
China, 20, 25, 34, 45, 55, 60, 63-5, 82-5, 108, 112, 115, 131, 134
China lobby, 84
Churchill, Winston, 28, 31, 33, 83, 102
civil rights (*see also* blacks), 42-4, 70-4, 94-7, 122-3
Civilian Conservation Corps, 10, 11
Clean Air Act (1970), 124
Clifford, Clark M., 46, 132
Cochinos Bay, *see* Bay of Pigs
Cohen, Benjamin, 18
Committee to Defend America by Aiding the Allies, 23
Committee to Re-elect the President (CREEP), 125
Connor, Eugene 'Bull', 95
Consumer Product Safety Act (1972), 124
Coolidge, Calvin, 1
Cooper v. Aaron, 73
Corcoran, Thomas, 18
Coughlin, Father Charles E., 12
Council of Economic Advisers, 40
Cuba, 104
    Bay of Pigs, 106-8
    missile crisis, 109-12
Czechoslovakia, 59, 117, 154

Davis, John W., 12
Dean, John, 125
Democratic Party, 8, 12, 38-9, 68, 93-4, 98-9
Diem, Ngo Dinh, 83, 113, 114
Dienbienphu, 82
Dukakis, Michael, 149
Dulles, Allen, 107
Dulles, John Foster, 79-81, 83, 88, 131

Eastern Europe, 21, 30-3, 53-5
Economic Opportunity Act (1964), 97-8
Economic Recovery Tax Act (1981), 146
Eden, Anthony, 86
Eisenhower, Dwight D.
    CIA operations, 85-6
    civil rights, 70-4
    defence spending, 74-5
    economic growth under, 75-7
    election of 1952, 67-8
    Farewell Address, 75, 145
    Indochina, 82-3
    Kennedy succession, 104
    Korean armistice, 81-2
    legislation under, 68-9
    limited war, 65
    McCarthyism, 49
    nuclear weapons, 81-2
    partnership with Dulles, 79-81
    Quemoy and Matsu islands, 84-5
    relations with Khrushchev, 90-2
    Soviet rapprochement, 88-92
    Suez crisis, 86-7
Egypt, 86-7
El Salvador, 149-50
employment, 5, 10, 26, 38
Employment Act (Full Employment Bill), 39
Erlichman, John, 125
Erlin, Sam J., 72, 125
Ethiopia, 139
European Recovery Plan (Marshall Plan), 58-9, 74

Fair Employment Practices Committee, 27, 43
Family Assistance Plan (FAP), 123
Farm Credit Administration (FCA), 10
Faubus, Governor Orval, 72-3
Federal Emergency Relief Administration (FERA), 10

Federal Home Loan Bank Act (1932), 9

Federal Housing Administration, 11

Finland, 21

Ford, Gerald, 120-1, 126-7, 138, 144

France, 20, 82-3, 119

Friedman, Milton, 143

Gaither Report, 74

Galbraith, John K., 3, 11, 93

Gayle v. Browder (1956), 73

Geneva
    arms talks, 90-1
    conference of 1954, 83
    summit of 1955, 89
    summit: Gorbachev and Reagan, 153

Germany (West), 20-3, 27, 28, 32-3, 52-3, 58-60, 77, 90, 108, 119, 131, 136, 154

Goldwater, Sen. Barry, 98

Gorbachev, Mikhail, 153-4

Gramm-Rudman-Hollings Act (1985), 147-8

Great Britain, 20, 33-4, 119

Greece, 56-7

Grenada, 151

Guatemala, 85-6, 107

Habib, Philip, 152

Haldeman, H. R., 125

HARDTACK, 90

Haynsworth, Clement F., 123

Helsinki Accords, 136

Hiss, Alger, 46

Hitler, Adolf, 20, 25

Hoover, Herbert, 5-7, 9, 17

Hopkins, Harry, 18

Housing and Urban Development Act (1965), 99

Hughes, Charles E., 15

Hull, Cordell, 29

Humphrey, George, 81

Humphrey, Hubert H., 117, 121-2

Hungary, 87-9, 154

Indochina (*see also* Vietnam), 25, 34, 82, 91

Intermediate Nuclear Forces (INF), 153-4

Interstate Highways Act (1956), 69

Iran, 85, 128, 138, 140-1

Iran-Contra affair, 150-1

Israel, 86, 137, 151-2

Japan, 20, 21, 25, 26, 27, 34-5, 52, 55, 62, 65, 77, 119-20, 131, 133

Jaworski, Leon, 126

Johnson, Lyndon B.
    assessment of Great Society, 102
    civil rights, 96-7
    election of 1968, 116-17, 121
    Vietnam war, 113-16
    war on poverty, 97-9

Kennan, George, F., 56

Kennedy, Edward, 145

Kennedy, John F.
    assassination, 97, 112
    Bay of Pigs, 106-8
    Berlin problem, 108-9
    civil rights, 94-7
    Cuban missile crisis, 109-11
    defence, 105-7
    election of 1960, 77, 93-4, 104-5
    inaugural address, 94, 104

Kennedy, Robert F., 94, 116

Khomeini, Ayatollah, 140-1

Khrushchev, Nikita, 88, 90-1, 108, 110

King, Rev. Martin Luther, 73-4, 94-6, 100-1

Kissinger, Henry, 126, 131-7

Korea, 139

Korean War, 49, 62-5, 67, 74, 82

Kreuger, Ivar, 6

Kristol, Irving, 143-4

Ky, Nguyen Cao, 114

labour, 11-12, 38-42
Laffer, Arthur, 143
Laos, 133-4
Lebanon, 87, 151
Lend-Lease, 24, 29
Leuchtenburg, William E., 1, 18
Lewis, John L., 40
Little Rock, crisis at, 72-3
Long, Huey P., 12
Lowi, Theodore, 18
Loyalty Review Board, 47
Lumumba, Patrice, 85

MacArthur, General Douglas, 63
McCarthy, Sen. Eugene, 116
McCarthy, Sen. Joseph, 45, 48-9, 88
    and McCarthyism, 38, 45-50
McCord, James W., 125
McGovern, Sen. George, 124-5
McLaurin v. Oklahoma State Regents,
    44
McNamara, Robert S., 94, 105, 109,
    111, 117
Mao Zedong, 60, 112, 136
Marshall, Burke, 95
Marshall, George, 48, 56, 58-9
    Marshall Plan, *see* European
        Recovery Plan
Mexico, 150
Milliken v. Bradley (1974), 122
Mine Safety and Health Act (1970),
    124
Minh, Ho Chi, 82
Mitchell, John N., 125
Moley, Raymond, 18
Mollet, Guy, 86
Montgomery, Alabama
    bus boycott, 73, 94
Moral Majority, 144
Morgan, John P., 6
Morgenthau, Henry, 33
Mossadeq, Mohammed, 49, 85, 140

Moynihan, Daniel, 102
Mulford v. Smith (1939), 16
Mussolini, Benito, 20
My Lai, 132

Nagy, Imre, 87-8
Nasser, Gamel Abdel, 86
National Association for the Advance-
    ment of Colored People (NAACP),
    43
National Defense Education Act
    (1958), 69
National Environmental Policy Act
    (1970), 124
National Labor Relations Board, 11,
    41
*National Labor Relations Board v.
    Laughlin Steel Corporation* (1937),
    16
National Recovery Administration
    (NRA), 10
Neutrality Act (1935-1937), 21, 22,
    23, 24
New Deal, 8-19, 37, 40, 44-5, 49, 68,
    120, 128, 143, 146, 148 *see also*
    individual agencies
New Look, 81
Nicaragua, 149
Nitze, Paul, 61
Nixon, Richard M.
    arms agreements, 135-6
    China visit, 134-5
    civil rights, 122
    economic policy, 123-4
    election of 1968, 121-2
    McCarthyism, 46, 49
    Middle East, 137-8
    presidential candidate (1960),
        93-4
    Supreme Court, 122-3
    Vietnam war, 117, 131-4
    Watergate crisis, 125-7
Nomura, Kichisaburo, 25
North, Oliver, 150

North Atlantic Treaty Organization
(NATO), 50, 61, 80, 88, 117
North Korea, *see* Korean War
NSC-68, 61-2, 65, 74

Occupational Safety and Health Act
(1970), 124
Office of Price Administration, 37
Office of Production Management,
24
Olympic Games, 140
Omnibus Budget and Reconciliation
Act (1981), 146
Organization for Afro-American
Unity, 101
Organization of Petroleum Exporting
Countries (OPEC), 120
Oswald, Lee Harvey, 97

Palestinians, 137, 151-2
Panama Canal, 138
Parks, Rosa, 73
Peace Corps, 111
Pentagon Papers, 132
Pleiku, 114
Podhoretz, Norman, 144
Poindexter, John, 150
Poland, 21, 30-2, 55, 154
Potsdam Conference, 32
Powell, Lewis, 123
Powers, Gary, 91
Public Works Administration, 10

Ray, James Earl, 101
Reagan, Ronald
central American policy, 149-51,
152
conservatism and 1980 election,
144-6
government spending, 146-9
Iran, hostage crisis, 141
Middle East, 151-2
presidential nomination (1976),
127

relations with Soviets, 152-4
Reconstruction Finance Corporation,
5, 9, 68
Regan, Donald, 151
Rehnquist, William, 123
Republican Party, 9, 13, 38, 67-8,
79-81, 121-3
Reykjavik Summit, 153
Rhee, Syngman, 62
Richardson, Elliot, 126
Ricks, Willie, 101
Ridgway, General Matthew, 65
Roosevelt, Franklin, D., 4, 5, 146
coming of Second World War,
22-6
elections, 8-9
federalism, 14
neutrality, 21-4
New Deal, 10-19; *see also
individual agencies*
Poland, 30-2
presidential office, 17-19
Soviet Union, 28-35
Supreme Court, 15-17
Roosevelt, Kermit, 85
Ruckelshaus, William, 126
Rusk, Dean, 131
Russell, Richard, 72

St Lawrence Seaway Act (1954), 69-
70
Sandinistas, 149-50
*Schechter Poultry Corporation v.
United States* (1935), 15
Schlesinger, Arthur M. Jnr., 107
Second Front, 28-9
Second World War, 20-35, 52-3, 63,
154
Securities Exchange Act (1935), 11
Sinai Desert, 137
Sinclair, Upton, 12
Sirica, John, J., 125
Smith, Al, 12
Social Security Act, 11, 69, 70

South-East Asia Treaty Organization (SEATO), 83
South Korea, *see* Korea
Southern Christian Leadership Conference (SCLC), 73
Soviet Union, 7, 21, 28, 30-5, 46, 52-66, 79-80, 85-92, 105-6, 108-11, 117, 131, 134-41, 152-4
Spanish Civil War, 20
Sputnik, 50, 89-90
Stalin, Josef, 30-4, 59, 79, 88; *see also* Soviet Union
Stevenson, Adlai E., 67-8
Stewart Machine Company v. Davis (1937), 16
Stimson, Henry L., 24, 35
Stock Market
crash of 1929, 2-4
Strategic Arms Limitation Talks (SALT), 135, 139-40
Strategic Defense Initiative (SDI), 153
Suez Crisis, 86-7, 89
Supreme Court, 15, 16, 44, 71-3, 122-3, 144
Swann v. Charlotte-Mecklenburg Board of Education (1971), 122
Sweatt v. Painter (1950), 44

Taft, Robert, 41, 67
Taft-Hartley Act 41-2
Taiwan (Formosa), 84, 136-7
Tennessee Valley Authority (TVA), 10
Tet Offensive, 115-16
Thieu, Nguyen, 114
Tho, Le Duc, 133
Tonkin Gulf, 114, 133
Tower, John, 151
Truman, Harry S.
and Eisenhower, 79-80
atomic bomb, 35, 54
Chinese civil war, 60
civil rights, 42-4, 70

defence and *NSC-68*, 61-2
election of 1952, 67
European Recovery Plan, 58-9
Fair Deal, 44-5
full employment, 39-40
Korean war, 62-5
labour, 39-42
McCarthyism, 45-9
political style, 38
post-war order, 52-3
Soviet Union, 52-66
Truman Doctrine, 56-7, 74, 138
Tugwell, Rexford G., 18

unemployment, *see* employment
United Nations, 30, 64
United States v. Butler (1936), 15
United States v. New York Times (1972), 132
United States v. Nixon (1974), 126

Vance, Cyrus, 139
Vietcong, *see* Vietnam
Vietnam, 83, 99, 108, 112-17, 119, 132-4; *see also* Indochina

Wallace, George C., 121-2, 124-5
Wallace, Henry, 47
War Production Board, 24
Warren, Earl, 71
Warsaw Pact, 88
Warsaw Uprising, 32
Watergate, 125-7, 129, 137
Works Progress Administration (WPA), 11

X, Malcolm, 101

Yalta Conference, 32-4, 46
Yom Kippur War (1973), 110, 120, 137

Zhou Enlai, 136